Contemporary Housing

Maria Alessandra Segantini

Contemporary Housing

Editor
Luca Molinari

Design
Marcello Francone

Editing
Doriana Comerlati

Layout
Paola Ranzini

Translations
Robert Burns for Language
Consulting Congressi S.r.l.,
Milan

Iconographical Research
Alessandra Mion
Maria Alessandra Segantini
with Claudia Zanda

Editors of the Project Entries
Claudia Zanda
and Roberta Osta

First published in Italy
in 2008 by
Skira Editore S.p.A.
Palazzo Casati Stampa
via Torino 61
20123 Milano
Italy
www.skira.net

Printed and bound in Italy.
First edition

ISBN 978-88-6130-535-9

Distributed in North America by
Rizzoli International Publications,
Inc., 300 Park Avenue South,
New York, NY 10010, USA.
Distributed elsewhere
in the world by Thames
and Hudson Ltd.,
181A High Holborn,
London WC1V 7QX,
United Kingdom.

Photographic Credits
Ábalos & Herreros
Architects, Madrid. Photo
Paolo Roselli
Aires Mateus, Lisbon. Photo
© DMF – Lisbon (Rights
Reserved)
Benno Albrecht
Aranguren+Gallegos
Architects
Alejandro Aravena. Photo
C. Palma
Architectural Office Marlies
Rohmer. Photo R. Aldershoff,
R. Schipper, R. van Rijthoven
Architectures Jean Nouvel.
Photo Philippe Ruault
© Architectuurstudio HH.
Photo Babette Wijsman,
Jens Willebrand
Wiel Arets Architects. Wiel
Arets, Bettina Kraus, Philippe
Dirix, Mai Henriksen. Photo
Jan Bitter
Atelier Bow-Wow. Photo
S. Hiraga
Auer+Weber. Photo Roland
Halbe
Baumschlager-Eberle. Photo
Eduard Hueber
Beckmann-n'Thépé Agency
and Associates. Photo Bruno
Fert, Stephan Lucas
Bolles+Wilson. Photo
Christian Richters
Botticini Architetti. Photo
G. Rasia dal Polo
Gonçalo Byrne Arquitectos.
Photo Fernando and Sergio
Guerra
C+S ASSOCIATI. Carlo
Cappai, Maria Alessandra
Segantini. Photo Carlo
Cappai, Marco Zanta, Pietro
Savorelli
Calori Azimi Botineau (CAB)
Architects. Photo Serge
Demailly
Carmassi Studio Architettura.
Photo Mario Ciampi
David Chipperfield Architects.
Photo Christian Richters
Claus en Kaan Architecten.
Photo Christian Richters,
Luuk Kramer

Coop Himmelb(l)au. Photo
Peter Korrak, Gerald
Zugmann, Alexander Koller
Dellekamp Arquitectos.
Photo Oscar Necoechea
Delugan Meissl Associated
Architects. Photo Margherita
Spiluttini
Diener & Diener Architekten.
Photo Christian Richters
E2A. Photo Andreas Rubin,
Michael Freisager, Tobias
Madorin, Felix Frei
Peter Ebner, Günter
Eckerstorfer. Photo
Margherita Spiluttini
Carlos Ferrater Partnership.
Photo Alejo Bagué
Andreas Fuhrimann and
Gabrielle Hächler Architects
Gigon/Guyer Architekten.
Photo Harald F. Müller,
Heinrich Helfenstein
Herzog & de Meuron. Photo
Margherita Spiluttini
Hillebrandt, Schultz -
Architektur. Photo Christian
Richters
Steven Holl Architects.
Image © Andy Ryan, © Paul
Warchol
Holz Box Tirol, Erich Strolz.
Photo G.R. Weet
KCAP. Photo Rob't Hart, Jan
Bitter
Hans Kollhoff. Photo Studio
Nemec
Josep Lluís Mateo MAP
Architects. Photo Duccio
Malagamba, Xavier Ribas,
Daria Scagliola
Mecanoo architects. Photo
Christian Richters
Metrogramma. Photo Filippo
Romano and Daniel Bellini
MGM.Mariscal.Giles.Mariscal.
Architectos. Photo Fernando
Alda, Hisao Suzuki
MVRDV. Photo Rob't Hart
Ryue Nishizawa
OFIS. Photo Tomaz Gregoric
Sergio Pascolo. Photo Roland
Halbe
OMA. Image Courtesy of the
Office for Metropolitan

Architecture (OMA). Photo
Hans Werleman
Helena Paver Nijric. Photo
F. Orsenigo, D. Kalogjera
PK Arkitektar Ehf. Photo
Rafael Pinho, Helge Garke
Pastor Architetti Associati.
Photo M. Michelozzo Pastor
Wolfram Popp-Planungen
Architekt BDA. Photo Stefan
Meyer
Georg W. Reinberg. Photo
R. Steiner
Kazuyo Sejima & Associates.
Photo Shinkenchiku-sha
Eduardo Souto de Moura.
Photo Luis Ferreira Alves
Studio 3X Nielsen. Photo
I. Mjell
Studio Bertani Vezzali. Photo
Paola De Pietri, Archivio
Ufficio Progetti
Studio Camerana & Partners.
Photo © Bruna Biamino,
© Reinhard Görner
Studio Canali. Photo Guido
Canali
Studio Cristofani & Lelli
architetti. Photo Mario
Ciampi, Alberto Muciaccia
Studio Fuksas. Carlo
Valsecchi fotografo
Studio Cherubino
Gambardella
Studio Iotti-Pavarani. Photo,
iotti + pavarani
Studio Ludens
Studio Pellegrini. Photo Mario
Ciampi, Pietro Savorelli
Studio Zucchi Architetti
UdA ufficio di architettura.
Photo A. Ferrero
UN Studio. Photo Christian
Richters
Van den Oever-Zaaijer & P
Architecten
Erick van Egeraat. Photo
Christian Richters
Hans Peter Wörndl Architect.
Photo Paul Ott
Riken Yamamoto & Field
Shop. Photo Tomio Ohashi,
Jan Dominik Geipel

Contents

The Home: Threshold between Private and Collective Space
Maria Alessandra Segantini

The home, great protagonist of modern architecture, was the main testing grounds for urban experimentation for much of the past century.

At the end of World War I, with Europe forced to redraw its economic and political geography, possible new housing models became central elements of thought, discussion and proposals. All the major European cities got the intelligentsia of international architecture involved in the issue: Jacobus Johannes Oud in Rotterdam, Ernst May in Frankfurt, and Tony Garnier in Lyon, just to name a few.

In 1925, Ludwig Mies van der Rohe was hired by the German Werkbund to develop a master plan for the 1927 Stuttgart exposition. He invited seventeen other European architects each to develop housing prototypes. Among others, the projects by Mies and Le Corbusier constituted a sort of manifesto of *Befreites Wohnen* (liberated living) as famously defined by Siegfried Giedion. The experience of the Weissenhof Estate ushered in the Congrès Internationaux d'Architecture Moderne (CIAM), whose 1929 edition, "Housing for an Existential Minimum", addressed new concepts in housing and also led to the organization of exhibitions in Wrocław, Zurich and Stockholm. The exemplars built for the Baba Housing Estate in Prague still stand as landmarks for Czech architects.

The precepts of a new functional architecture spread throughout Europe. The post-WWII reconstruction plans often moved along lines that were openly antithetical, with the intensive construction of "housing machines" and prefabricated structures on the one hand, and the development of models more strongly associated with local tradition (as in Le Havre or Rome) and the New Towns of the Anglo-Saxon and Scandinavian countries, on the other.

The project in Boulevard Michelet in Marseilles, an evolution of Le Corbusier's theories implicit in the 1922 Immeuble Villas, unites the concepts of functionality, standardization, communal infrastructure, vertical *cité-jardin*, and *modulor* into a revolutionary manifesto of a new approach to the design of housing and cities. From the Unité d'Habitation to the German Siedlungen, from the Amsterdam plan to the Frankfurt kitchen, a positivist egalitarianism raised the primary needs of the individual to a collective value on all scales, seeking a universal response to the miserable conditions of metropolitan slums.

Functionality and standardization, minimal spaces and services, constituted the bases of the programmes initiated in every country to offer a housing *ration*[1] sized to fit the nuclear family and responding to the quite serious problems of overcrowding and substandard hygiene.

In Great Britain, reconstruction strategies took form during World War II with the presentation in 1942 of a model for the development of London. This model would find implementation four years later in the New Towns Act. The British New Towns oscillated between vernacular solutions and proposals aligned with examples of modern architecture, where the sincerity of the functional organization and "truth to materials" – to use the phrase coined by Reyner Banham – are expressed in a straightforward manner on building exteriors in the architecture of New Brutalism.

Sweden took its cues from the Anglo-Saxon model. The Swedish social democratic tradition adopted and developed the English New Towns by anchoring them – as in the best known example of Vallingby, west of Stockholm, with the project coordinated by Sven Markelius – to an efficient transportation system as well as to a decentralized organization of principal public services (schools, social centres, municipal services) supporting nuclei composed of 6,000 inhabitants. This project became a sort of manifesto for a policy based on public rather than market management of urban development. The New Town thus stands in antithesis to the speculative model for developing urban land, emphasizing the need to work with collective spaces and the landscape, anticipating themes that still arouse particular interest today.

In Holland, a model country for habitational excellence, the post-WWII period witnessed the implementation of a plan to set aside thirty percent of residential space for public initiative low-income housing. This resulted in the construction of compact developments/systems linked up with infrastructure and services.

In Italy, the Fanfani Plan established INA-Casa in 1949, a broad-reaching programme calling for commitment among social and economic policymakers – perhaps for the last time with a unified intention on the national scale – to address and resolve the problem of unemployment via the development of the construction sector. This programme offered work to a large number of architects and workers and resulted in the construction of solid and efficient structures.[2] Opposed by certain segments of architectural critics, who described Quaroni and Ridolfi's Tiburtino station as an "alienating antidote" that takes refuge in "rigorous grids or the geometric terrorism of the Neue Sachlichkeit",[3] the plan was designed by Adalberto Libera following a line that promoted a process of urbanization under the banner of low population density, green space, and forms divorced from rationalism constructed in respect for local traditions and materials. Giving concrete expression to the theories expounded by Gio Ponti in his "casa esatta e per tutti" (precise house for everyone), the INA-Casa Plan united social solidarity and architectural evolution in Italy. We Italians are now the heirs of this legacy but incapable of undertaking an effective process of imbuing it with new qualities and making it a current reality.

Clearly influenced by the functionalist and post-functionalist pursuits and models that guided the housing revolution in modern architecture, contemporary thinking and projects on the theme of housing bandy the outcomes of these experiments about, having nevertheless abandoned the desire to offer a universal response to primary human needs.

This volume has been conceived as a collection of some one hundred meaningful projects from the past ten years. It has been divided into six chapters – *density, sustainability, transforming, developing, inhabiting, reinhabiting* – with the idea of singling each of them out in order to clarify the interpretation of some of the themes underpinning one line of thought on contemporary housing planning and design.

The issue of *density* has recently acquired new impetus and relevance in collective housing design, as we see in projects ranging from MVRDV's work in Amsterdam to Steven Holl's Japanese structures. High density housing has overcome the initial resistance to the sorts of large containers that appeared in the 1960s with the objective of improving the individual's living conditions, but which only ended up addressing a generic, standardized user, who was the product both of the utopias professed by those with boundless faith in prefab building techniques and of socialist ideology.

Flexibility and prefabrication became the pivotal themes in housing projects addressing the needs of a society characterized by rapidly and continuously changing models of habitation. From Moshe Safdie's Habitat 67 to Yona Friedman's models for Israel, from the pneumatic structures of the Haus-Rucker-Co group in Austria to the Spiral City and famous Nakagin Capsule Tower by Kisho Kurokawa in Japan, from Paul Maymont's Ville Flottante in France and Archigram's Plug-In City in Great Britain to the No-Stop City and the Residential Diagrams of the Florentine group Archizoom and John Habraken's theoretical interpretations, it was believed that the concept of variability could become a concrete reality by applying the capacity of industrial production and standardization to a framework that guaranteed a sense of unity for the project in its juxtaposition with the city.

On the ideological side, the organization of the peripheral areas in socialist Europe witnessed the application of heavy prefab construction techniques (*Plattenbau*) and thus became the expression of the State's desire to ensure housing for the entire labour class. The sheer size of the superstructure was inevitably fated to devalue the qualities of the individual and the landscape, a loss in value that is still clearly evident in the examples of Corviale, the later Spanish work of Ricardo Bofill, or the *grands ensembles* in France.

After the collapse of both ideological matrices and the eclipse of the ideals of the Modern Movement, the conflict between housing and the city became more acute, expressed through a quest for a stronger relationship with nature, bringing about the phenomenon of the *città della dispersione* (urban sprawl), where the single family dwelling becomes the protagonist in a one-dimensional development and the garden and living quarters, both private property, are incapable of creating a sociability that extends beyond the legally recognized boundaries.

In this sense, the high-density collective housing project embodies a response to the need and desire to confront empty space, the space of the city and the community. Land is conserved so that it can be used in a different and more diversified way and so that its usage options and availability can be maximized. Housing density and collective space become two elements in a reciprocal tension that we see most clearly in special building projects – university student housing or housing for special categories

– where the housing, precisely because it is minimal or highly specialized, stands in a precise relation to collective space. It requires the presence of this collective space while at the same time being necessary for bringing life to it. In this type of housing system, there are spaces that filter access to the individual dwellings, with running balconies for circulation and common/social areas, and generously dimensioned open-use spaces that attract the interest of the local community. These are informal spaces that can be adapted and shaped by those living there.

In the projects by Mateo, Aires Mateus, Steven Holl, Auer+Weber, KCAP, and Claus en Kaan, the vivacity of the collective space, whether given a specific functional characterization or dedicated to circulation and distribution, becomes a necessary element to complement the minimal dimensions dedicated to the individual housing unit.

On the other hand, as we see in the Spinnerei of Leipzig, it is precisely the contiguity between artist housing and the exhibition and collective space of the large redeveloped industrial complex that gives substance and quality to the act of displaying art, while a part of the factory is simultaneously inhabited and used for producing art.

What role must be regained by collective space? From the inhabitants of Dharavi, the biggest slum in Mombai, to those in Cairo, still today some communities support themselves by means of an informal economy grounded in the informal exploitation of the collective spaces they have appropriated and transformed, using, for example, the space under a bridge as a grand hall for the parties of an entire neighbourhood.[4]

Collective space in this sense is enriched by the potential to become an interchange space open to multiculturalism.

In Herman Hertzberger's project for the Rotterdamerstrasse complex, part of an ideal continuum with the earlier Scandinavian work of Ralph Erskine and the theories and creations of Team 10, a large central court enclosed by grassy embankments, an informal plot with no specific functional characterization, becomes a collective space of excellence for the community living within the enclosure. It stands in opposition to the punctiform urban pattern of single-family dwellings and proposes a housing model that exalts the scale of the individual precisely in recognizing the individual as an inhabitant of a collective space.

On the other hand, contemporary concern for a new housing density, in response to the urban sprawl that results in an almost totally human-transformed landscape, is generally linked to considerations regarding land use, not least of which is the call for education and consciousness-raising with regard to the sustainable use of our planet's resources.

Optimization of service distribution, a lessening of pressure on agricultural lands, reduction in the need to commute and/or travel using autonomous means coupled with promotion of public transportation, and flexibility of housing space are only some of the themes embodied in the values of sustainable development. Just to cite a few figures, 60 housing units per hectare are necessary to make the construction of a streetcar line economically sustainable, and the average housing density in the major European cities is 93 housing units per hectare.[5]

The theme of the *sustainability* of housing projects is assuming increasing importance and beginning to shape actions and choices in the market. In Holland, the 1992 Building Decree obliges planners and architects to address the issues of energy savings and thermal and acoustic insulation in building design. Most countries have adopted regulations or guidelines in line with the Kyoto Protocol. Once again the field of collective housing appears to be a central area of research and development, precisely because experiments can be carried out in this sector over a wide scale and at relatively low cost.

Some of the most significant examples are found in the architectural work of the Baumschlager & Eberle studio in Austria. The studio has a tradition of promoting energy savings, alternative energy resources and reduced operating costs in their projects, designing compact buildings with highly specialized shells. Their facades are filters that can be completely opened or closed to the outdoors depending on seasonal climate conditions.

The theme of *sustainability* is certainly also associated with that of transformability and flexibility. These terms no longer refer to structural modifications to the house, but rather to the development of a basic structure that can accommodate a range of possible transformations. In a certain sense this takes us beyond the long process of research and development that focused its efforts on the question of building type while abandoning the technological illusion of prefabricated buildings.

The term "flexibility" applied to housing now seems to have transposed itself from the individual dwelling to the city. It is no longer attributed to the possible technological or distributive modifications of internal space, but rather associated with the possibility of being able to move across town, change job or place of residence in a sort of compulsory or desired nomadism, where the house becomes more strongly identified with the place where one carries out productive activities, often an office where one sleeps, sometimes a space where one works.[6]

The theme of flexibility is choreographed against different backdrops. Examples include projects for the Nishigawa housing in Tianjin, China, in 2003, composed of a cluster of rooms without circulation or distribution spaces, or the programme of the Chilean Alejandro Aravena for Quinta Monroy, which produces a model of subsidized housing that can be expanded over time depending on the needs of a potentially changing family. Each house has direct access to collective spaces.

The market itself offers a model for this type of demand that translates into a *prêt-à-porter* response, into an increasingly decisive desire for "customization" by users. Just as they *inhabit* Second Life, these users *connect* for only a few hours with their houses. They can modify it to suit their tastes and whims by acquiring Ikea-type furnishing elements to be installed in an "open floor plan" whose virtual properties can be modified with the speed of a mouse click. The users are coddled by a market that manipulates the role and the value of architecture, giving it the allure of a successful brand claiming kinship to the most sensational projects. Among these we mention the housing towers of Santiago Calatrava on the banks of the East River in Manhattan, which set out twelve glass cubes, twelve urban buildings suspended from a central structure.

The model that seems to gain currency today is thus that of a sort of "adaptable residence", compact in design to save land but incapable of confronting and embracing such issues as diversity, emergence, collectivity, community.

What immediately surfaces is the weakness of a landscape that seeks definition only as an internal landscape, customized by the individual and his or her movements in space but which, replicated in infinite micro-variables, turns out to be incapable of extending itself into and confronting the city. The "desire for belonging to a specific place and a specific society seems to increase steadily as the figure of the global nomad – who turns out, almost without exception, to be a social and intellectual monster – becomes the hero of future life".[7] The reasoning revolves around the terms of duration and "urban structure" that Hans Kollhoff uses to oppose the mere functionalist concept of the dwelling: "Buildings have to be built to last for generations. They have to age well to provide future testimony to a collective memory and to become part of a city's history."[8]

This is part of the vision that underpins the work of architects such as Hans Kollhoff, Mecanoo, Claus en Kaan, Fritz van Dongen, and Massimo Carmassi. They work with an architecture that seeks to "build the fabric": "The skeleton of the city is our objective, and certainly not the formulation of offbeat images that are excogitated solely for the sake of being original. Our task is to design and build the norm and not the exception."[9]

We have thus chosen to dedicate a chapter to the thinking and specificity of the place or context.

Regarding the theme of the interplay between urban morphology and building type, the 1980s and 1990s re-established the links between housing and urban redevelopment.

In 1988 a long planning process was initiated in Holland to redevelop the Eastern Harbour Docklands of Amsterdam, built on land reclaimed from the sea, or *polders* as the Dutch call them. This was followed by the well-known development of the islands of Java and Borneo-Sporenburg designed by West 8, who established an in-line model with homogeneous density but capable of the greatest possible variations in aggregation of the facades giving onto the canals and of the building units giving onto internal patios.

In 1987 Josef Paul Kleihues was hired by the International Building Exhibition (IBA) organizers in Berlin, where he proposed a sort of "city repair" and picked up the design of the nineteenth-century block with an internal courtyard in response to the wreckage wreaked across the landscape by dispersed construction work. Aldo Rossi, Oswald Mathias Ungers, Rob Krier, Hans Kollhoff, and Arata Isozaki are only a few of the protagonists whose proposals are directed toward offering a durable structure to the city.

These models appeared to be both easily comprehensible and exportable, and made substantial inroads into housing markets, especially in countries like Italy where the theme of housing for many years carried no social-political weight or interest for architects or planners. Here the notion of context was devalued and reduced to banal mimicry of pre-existing architectural elements in terms of style, an approach that was crystallized in the normative apparatus.

A renewed interest in the specificity of the context and in the possibilities associated with this type of approach suggested a possible response to a generalized global vision of inhabiting the house and the city. Here, the importance of concepts such as the ground-building interface is newly emphasized, almost as the material expression of the house's need to belong to the specific landscape in which it is set, going far beyond the simplistic approach of dressing up a standardized model in new clothes. "Barbie's clothes are like the skin of domestic architecture, a wardrobe to dress up an idealised typology and standardised functions."[10]

The examples collected in the chapter dedicated to the theme of *inhabiting* also seem to reflect on the terms of the question in a refined way, especially when they refer to those which Pierluigi Nicolin interprets as a second order of meanings, expressive meanings with respect to the functionalist invariant that still persist in housing production,[11] meanings that regard project quality, image and identity.

The housing project currently finds itself, in the best of international production, having to work with the space that defines the section and boundary between inside and outside – the enclosure, in physical terms, and the collective spaces in terms of possibilities. In spite of the noteworthy market production that disconnects the process of organizing interior space from that of the design of the *maquillage* of the external walls, in the selected projects we do not observe a true opposition between indoors and outdoors, between spatial organization liberated from the functionalist need to project itself without qualification into the exterior and building image, between "customizable" space and "cosmetic" space, as the building shell is often interpreted in today's most fashionable solutions. What we see, rather, is more of a dialectic, capable of working on the section of the threshold determined by the enclosure of the housing unit, at the boundary between inside and outside, which both establishes a relationship between individual and city and protects the individual from the city. The shell/threshold represents a space that can be expanded, as in the building in Barceloneta with its louver-blinds, to contain loggias or windows. It can extend indoors with seats or expand outwards with terraces, thus becoming a space for climate control and energy savings. It is a space that opens onto its surroundings or closes them off, composed of an organism that is capable of modifying itself at different times of day or night and in accordance with how it is used by the inhabitants. It is a space that can open in different ways to allow glimpses of its interior or close itself off completely to the city to defend the private dimension that Christopher Alexander sees as the primary condition of contemporary living.

The threshold addressed by the projects of Cino Zucchi, Calori Azimi Botineau, David Chipperfield, Carlos Ferrater, and Herzog & de Meuron in Paris establishes an agreement with the specificity of its context. It is a threshold crafted as a horizon, as a material, a section, a porous threshold framing sections of the landscape, that opens to welcome in light and life, whose object is the desire to recognize one's house as a home. "When I first came to live in this place I thought it would be but for a little space, but five years have already passed. This temporary hut of mine looks old and weather-beaten and on the roof the rotting leaves lie deep, while the moss has grown thick on the plastered wall. [...] It may be small, but there is room to sleep at night, and to sit down in the day-time, so that for one person there is no inconvenience."[12] With the construction of his house, initially intended to be provisory, Chomei alludes to the desire to obtain something lasting and durable and with it, a story. It is a threshold that in memory is a private but also a collective space, as we are taught by Joseph Kosuth's work of art in San Gimignano when he inscribed the stone of the Loggia del Podestà with this quote from Benjamin: "Là dove si può stare in piedi ci si può anche sedere. Non soltanto i bambini, ma anche le donne hanno il loro posto sulla soglia di casa a stretto contatto con la terra, le sue tradizioni e forse le sue divinità. La sedia davanti alla porta è già segno di innovazione cittadina" (Where you can stand you can also sit. Not just children, but women too have their place at the threshold of the house in close contact with the land, its traditions and perhaps its deities. The chair outside the door is already a sign of urban innovation).

A final thought regards the theme of *reuse*.

Alongside large-scale projects that revive and convert industrial facilities into housing units, the redevelopment of large harbour areas throughout Europe or entire prefabricated complexes in former East Germany re-establishes the individual human scale and becomes the representation of a new society, such as we see in the Stadtvillen in Leinefelde-Worbis. It seems that some of the projects presented in this section achieve a refined rewriting of inherited characteristics in a contemporary key. This is the case in Massimo Carmassi's designs for San Michele in Borgo. The building tradition and the city's collective memory become the materials of the project, which physically retraces the foundation plot of the old factory, rewriting it using modern wording merged with the constructive wisdom of tradition. It is a work destined to ferry the past into the present and conserve it through time.

The volume includes projects of different dimensions representing the complexity that we believe is still embodied in the word "inhabit". It is a dimension that registers the effects of globalization but seeks to offer some resistance in favour of the specificity of context, that seeks durability over immediate consumption, that seeks to save land by reinhabiting, densifying and also by applying discernment and awareness to the crafting of a building shell that is capable of lasting through time and acting as a porous membrane for climate control of the house. It is a dimension that works on the private threshold and on collective space with the objective of uniting the specificity of the project with the desire to offer an informal area that can be transformed into community space.

There are places where housing construction has been and continues to be an occasion for research and experimentation, nurtured and bolstered by a social-political tradition and awareness that sees it as an important item, as we see in Holland or northern European countries in general. In Italy, however, research into collective housing is still stopped – with the exception of a few specific local experiments – at the frontier of the Fanfani Plan.

Today, at a time when demand is sagging, the market seems more interested in investing in housing, even if recently it has put itself in the hands of the archistars, who are more useful for achieving greater volumes than for fostering new thinking about the dwelling and the city.

On the other hand, the tradition that recognizes the value of urban morphology, territorial stratification and concern for context, and draws its sustenance from the experiments of the protagonists of Italian architecture in the first half of the past century – from Luigi Moretti to Asnago/Vender or Gio Ponti, to name just a few – appears to offer fertile ground for reinvigorated discussion and research into specificity, without giving in to facile a-geographic mimicry exploiting the easy allure of passing fashion. The experience of Portello against CityLife in Milan is just one example – nevertheless absolutely efficacious – of this possible new, distinctly Italian approach, one which just may have enough power to refocus attention on the specificity of the project for housing in its dimension as node and threshold between individual and collective space.

[1] C. Aymonino (ed.), *L'abitazione razionale*, Padua: Marsilio, 1971.
[2] P. Di Biagi (ed.), *La grande ricostruzione. Il piano Ina-Casa e l'Italia degli anni cinquanta*, Rome: Donzelli, 2001.
[3] M. Tafuri, *Storia dell'architettura italiana*, Turin: Einaudi, 1986.
[4] M. Navarra, *Repairing Cities. Learning from Cairo*, Venice 2006.
[5] D. Rudlin, *Tomorrow. A Peaceful Path to Urban Reform. The Feasibility of Accommodating 75% of New Homes in Urban Areas*, London 1998.
[6] R. Sennett, "Capitalism and the City", in M. Echenique, A. Saint (eds.), *Cities of the New Millennium*, London-New York: Spon Press, 2001.
[7] H. Kollhoff, "Costruzione urbana contro alloggio", in *Lotus*, 94, 1997.
[8] Ibid.
[9] Ibid.
[10] X. Gonzales, "Barbie's New Clothes", in J. Mozas, A. Fernandez Per, *Density. New Collective Housing*, Vitoria-Gasteiz: a+t ediciones, 2006.
[11] P. Nicolin, "La funzione supplementare", in *Lotus*, 94, 1997.
[12] Kamo no Chomei, *The Ten Foot Hut and Tales of the Heike*, translated by A. L. Sadler, Sydney: Angus and Robertson, 1928.

Density

High-Density Collective Housing and Urban Space
Maria Claudia Clemente

High-density collective housing has for some time now returned as a central focus in international architectural culture after a period, one which has not actually ended yet, marked by hostility and aversion, almost by fear.

The recent work of MVRDV in Amsterdam and Madrid, Kazuyo Sejima's and Steven Holl's work in Japan, or Renzo Piano's high rise residential units, to name just a few, testify to a changed scenario. To get an understanding of how and why this is happening, what its principal characteristics are and what main changes have come about, a brief review of the situation is necessary so that we may comprehend the connotations and meanings of modern (twentieth-century) density and contemporary density, and their connotations within and relationships with the city space.

The Universal Individual
The large residential receptacles built in the first half of the twentieth century – from Le Corbusier's Unité d'Habitation and the German Siedlungen to the large residential units built in central and eastern Europe – were the expression of an ideal that was both illuminist and functionalist. Based on the principle of equality among individuals, it posited the needs of the individual as a social value. Starting from a principle of democracy and pursuing the objective of improving standards and conditions of living, the quest of planners in those years – of fundamental value in the growth and development of European cities – contributed strongly and positively to the elimination of differences and diversity among individuals. Like a sort of mass-produced product, the intended beneficiaries were individuals who ideally were "always equal", products of the values embodied in technological progress on the one hand and in socialist ideals on the other.

Subsequently, the *grands ensembles* in France, the austere containers of socialist Europe or the Brutalist buildings of Latin America, and the later example of the Corviale housing project in Rome were, each in their own way, offspring of the same mode of thinking. Although created on the basis of quite different needs and rationales – and no longer in the name of an ideal of universal progress – they were still conceived as a means of bringing well-being to increasingly broad segments of society by the application of industrial techniques of prefabrication, in which boundless faith was invested.

Large homogeneous containers, part of a series, neutral, abstract in their repetitiveness and mute in their abstraction; from the urban scale to the scale of the lodging, and from the zoning of the Amsterdam plan to the Frankfurt kitchen – the aversion for high-density residential units that has permeated and still permeates our society derives from images that are fascinating for their utopian and idealistic content, but reflect difficult and hostile conditions for those who actually had to live in them. This is mainly because once the utopia had faded, the utopian content revealed itself to be a glass-walled cage stifling personal expression.

In the mid 1990s, the cities of former East Germany – where architecture for much of the twentieth century was the concrete embodiment of a social model, and for this reason particularly emblematic – contained some 1.3 million empty apartments, entire deserted cities.[1] Following German reunification, thousands of people abandoned their houses to seek their personal space elsewhere, finding it in the single-family dwellings that were burgeoning in Germany in the same period.

Personal expression, the quest for a space of one's own, and also the pursuit of greater contact with nature have been among the main driving forces behind contemporary urban sprawl, beyond the boundless garden cities that have cannibalized the European territory.

Once the myth of infinite and universal progress had been debunked in western culture and socialist ideals had collapsed, people began searching for their own personal identity and path. This was the end of modernity as we knew it: a territory occupied by an infinite series of "equal (and identical) cities"[2] that affirm both the value of the individual but also his or her infinite and sublime solitude.

Designing the void: density and public spaces
But the thing that has not worked in modern and late-modern high-density collective housing (apart from the architecture) is the relationship with the open spaces of the city and the idea of community implicit in them. The ground was considered to be available land, like a huge backdrop against which to place figures, like a white sheet, a free and airy space, neutral and non-hierarchical, ample and available. It was not diversified, but homogeneous, like the society of equals it was intended for. It was an extended space, increasingly democratic but devoid of structure, episodic and fragmentary.

In Brasilia there is a lot of empty space but no public space. It is a fascinating *tabula rasa* but incapable of creating a sense of community. The density of the individual buildings corresponds to the idea of a rarefied, rational and organized city.

The experiments underway in the cities of former East Germany – Leipzig, Dresden, Cottbus, etc. – are extremely significant in this sense. The fury of demolition that was unleashed there, more than in any other European cities, proves that architecture is not the sole cause of depopulation. On the contrary, what is needed to revitalize the spaces of the city is a serious policy specific to them.[3]

Density and public space are thus two strongly interrelating elements, and this is not just because greater density means more collective space is available for the community, but also because the interaction between a building and the empty space around it can give the building itself a different theoretical foundation and meaning.

From the building to the city (toward a new density)
So why is it now necessary to go back to talking about density?

What does it mean today, and what do we look for in high-density residential buildings? What relationship is to be established with the city? What sense shall we give to empty spaces?

Density in the contemporary world has social, urban and environmental meanings. It results in a reduced consumption of land, the public asset *par excellence*. It optimizes resource use. It creates visual and symbolic nodes. It establishes landmarks in the city. Density does not necessarily mean the production of worthless junk.

A true topographic reduction appears increasingly necessary in large contemporary metropolises, which are being transformed into undistinguishable, unstructured megalopolises by the significant and widely recognized phenomenon of population movement toward the cities. They are cities that are now undergoing their own Modernity, a modernity without ideals, but which nevertheless attracts millions of people who are looking for an improved quality of life, a job, and more rights, exactly as happened in Europe in the twentieth century. We also have to look at these cities, while our European cities are becoming depopulated. And it is to these cities that we have to provide responses to the complex of questions that they raise.

In the age of the individual, the values that high-density residential buildings need to express are certainly different, as are the characteristics of the planning endeavour that gives concrete form and voice to words, concepts and meanings that emerged in the 1960s and 1970s and are now part of western architectural culture.

It was the pursuits of those decades, from the Situationists to the Archigram, from the Metabolists to the Radicals, which reacted to the domination of the modernist paradigm and brought the (unique) individual back into architectural culture, without translating it all into an abstract universal concept. On the contrary, it became an element of richness and multiplication of possibilities, a locus for experimentation and research.

The contemporary quest is now something that is well known and largely tried and tested. However, it is still worthwhile summarizing the principles that should guide a high-density residential project today.

These are:

On the scale of the single dwelling – flexibility of space, the capacity to transform over time and the potential for personalization.[4]

On the scale of the building – the definition of bona fide typological matrices capable of aggregating dwellings that differ from one another and responding to the diversity of demand not only in dimensional terms but also qualitatively, that is, to augment the possibilities and potentials for satisfying user needs.

In the internal distribution of the building – an increase in access paths, the rarefaction and opening of circulation spaces, the hybridization between circulation spaces and public spaces. In a word, to view distribution as a *promenade* and not as a simple functional connection.

Having got beyond the idea of the *common house* that guided so many modern projects (collective spaces, services, public spaces are to be sought in the city, a place for connection with the global world), it might be interesting to join the *dense house* with a minute fabric of spaces for work –offices, workshops – which in some cases may prove to be necessary for sustaining and ensuring the livelihood of a community.[5] Lastly, an increasingly important aspect is the search for a more organic relationship with nature: the presence of empty space as an environmental plus, the inclusion of natural spaces that can strengthen the relationship between indoors and outdoors, between the artificial dimension and the natural dimension, that transform the building into a socially and ecologically sustainable complex.

As heralded in the well-known 1981 project by the SITE group, *High-Rise of Home*,[6] which posed important questions for architectural culture, the high-density collective dwelling thus is transformed into a *dense individual house*, which is capable of answering the needs of the contemporary person while counterbalancing the city's tendency to expand outwards and all the phenomena associated with that expansion: consumption of land and resources, the necessary augmentation of the transport system, increased infrastructure requirements, etc.

If the dwelling and the building thus express a new individual trend, capable of absorbing and conveying the richness and complexity of contemporary society, the city space, the public space, is the space for *encountering others*. This is a need that remains unchanged in time and space.

A profusion of texts on the continuous city, on non-places, on circulation strategies have given the phenomenon of the consumption of territory an aura and an image. They offer cultured and fascinating explanations, but at the same time reflect a dulled – and in some cases cynical – acceptance of things as they are as something inevitable, because it is a condition and a process that cannot be planned. But perhaps the time has come to question this mindset using the instruments proper to architecture and urban design.

Public space: a possible definition
What idea of the city is needed to complement the dense individual house? What relation is there between density and public space?

There is a sort of ideal complementarity between density and public space: on the one hand, the awareness of a limit in the process of expansion of the city's territory makes density a real alternative to the phenomenon of metropolitan sprawl; on the other, the awareness of the need to limit the process of individualization attributes anew to the public space the function of a *locus* in which the system of relations among people and a dialogue with the community can be recomposed. As indeed the most recent research into urban space shows, the design of public space is the only area where the connotations of living in the city can be given new life.

It is difficult to provide an exact definition of public space. Is it to be identified by spatial characteristics? Can it be discerned from the design of the city or does it depend on immaterial or perhaps chance factors?[7]

Although public space can neither be considered a mere product of urban planning nor, much less, the simple space left over between two buildings, certain fundamental characteristics can nevertheless be defined.

First and foremost, it is *public*. In a city that is increasingly transformed by private actions – even over large portions of its territory[8] – it is increasingly important that the use and management of certain spaces remain within the purview of the community. This is the only way that "available space" can be conserved, space in which the so-called "use value" can be considered on a par with economic value. In other words, a space where shopping is not an absolute necessity but only one of a range of possible options.[9]

Public space has to allow the superimposition and concentration of different uses. The urban street is different from the country road.

In this sense, being "public" is a condition of the space that accommodates varying intensities and types of potential uses depending on the hour of the day, the weather conditions and also the passage of time. Public space allows itself to be exploited formally – thanks to equipment and fixtures – but also to be "occupied" informally. This is a fundamental characteristic because it highlights the semantic character of the space and the possibility that it can be interpreted in different ways. It is a space that does not impose behaviours on its occupants but one that is capable of inducing or eliciting attitudes. It is thus a differentiated space, a landscape, a piece of land[10] capable of holding together the built space and the void, a space that needs a different mindset from that associated with modernity. It is no longer a neutral sheet but a cluster,[11] a fabric. It is no longer homogeneous, but differentiated. It no longer contains indifferent voids but structured voids. It is no longer *a result*, but is itself *the subject* of the project. It is no longer rarefied emptiness but a density in itself, with a density of connotations, uses, and thus of meaning.

It is a *rewritable* space; but it is not a stage scene, nor a representation of the paradigm of the temporary, of the ideal of the nighttime event at all costs. Now the rage all over the planet, these nighttime parties betray the need for collective moments but at the same time the incapacity to transform the masses into a community. Public space is not a space conceived exclusively for being decorated or set up for specific purposes,[12] but rather a space that can absorb and be a backdrop for any decoration that is capable of transforming it, for any temporary and effective interpretation that modifies its use. It is a space that is capable over time of absorbing new social behaviours and new collective uses.

It is *accessible*, that is, it is not segregated, it is not divided, it is not controlled.

This question has a dual aspect: on the one hand, the problem of security from terrorist attack, a problem that affects rich western cities;[13] on the other, the multiplication of communities, which affects mainly Asian and South American megalopolises, in which the communities live in separate and autonomous clusters. In both cases, for the construction of a multiethnic society such as the one we live in, the thing that is very important is "the propagation of open, inviting and hospitable public spaces, which all categories of urban residents would be tempted to visit regularly and to share with others consciously and willingly" because "the 'fusion' required of reciprocal comprehension can only be the outcome of a *shared* experience; and sharing experiences is inconceivable without a shared space".[14]

It is a space that is able to transmit the value of a *civitas*, complex, multiethnic, open and transversal, but still a community, different from the way we knew it, a *civitas* constituted by a multiplicity of different individuals. "Is modernity our antiquity?" wonder the curators of the Documenta 12 exhibition in Kassel. Certainly, many ideals of modernity, such as "identity" and "culture" are still fully up to date and constitute the horizon for much of the world's population. Perhaps we need to give them some answers.

[1] See the extremely interesting catalogue for the exhibition: E. A. Busche, O. G. Hamm, P. C. Schmal, W. Voigt (ed. by), *NEU BAU LAND. Architecture and Urban Restructuring in Former East Germany*, Frankfurt am Main: E.A. Seeman, 2007.
[2] *La città uguale* [where *uguale* in Italian can mean both "equal" and "identical", thus "The equal/identical city", *translator's note*] is a project presented by Franco Purini at the 2000 architectural Biennale in Venice and published in M. Petranzan, G. Neri, *Franco Purini. La città uguale*, Padua: Il Poligrafico, 2005.
[3] In Cottbus, for example, the demolition not only did nothing to slow down the exodus but led to worsened land use and increased costs for constructing and operating infrastructure. In Leipzig, the philosophy "less density, more green" proved equally unsuccessful. On the other hand, the redesign of open spaces and green areas and the definition of social venues improved the quality of life and significantly reduced the exodus trend.
[4] This is so true that often real estate companies sell housing on paper in order to respond to specific requests and needs before the construction or even the design phases are completed.
[5] Dharavi, for example, the largest slum in Mumbai and in all of Asia, is self-supporting thanks to the informal economy that is active in its small dwellings. The main protest from Dharavi inhabitants regarding the possibility that the entire slum might be transformed into high-rise condominiums is precisely that of safeguarding the informal living and working conditions, as well as the neighbourly relations: "The people are questioning the established plan. If they go ahead with [the plan] it certainly will not benefit the community, the neighbourhood relations will be destroyed and what will happen is more or less what happens in America, where people are packed into high-density buildings at risk of rebellions and bloodshed, abandoned to the mercy of criminal activities [...] 45% of the people who live in Dharavi are micro-entrepreneurs [...] The informal economy is based on a cottage industry system, a dense network of workshops that may be no more than a single room [...] a culture of microbusinesses that generates a gross product of over 500 million euros..." From "Mumbai: Dharavi, Intervista con Jockin Arputham (National Slum Dwellers Federation)", in *Domus*, 2007.
[6] C. Toraldo di Francia (ed. by), *SITE architetture 1971–1988*, Roma: Officina Edizioni ,1989.
[7] A very interesting analysis of public space is found in W. Grasskamp, "Art and the City", in K. Bussmann, K. Konig, F. Matzner (ed. by), *Contemporary Sculpture. Projects in Münster 1997*, Stuttgart: Gerd Hatje, 1997.
[8] The new nodes introduced by the City

of Rome General Urban Planning Scheme (PRG) will be an interesting experiment in this respect. Will it be possible to create an *urban node* without the true participation of the public?

9 Quite interesting in this regard is the study of privately-owned public spaces in New York published in V. Tevere, "Privately Public", in S. Sheikh (ed. by), *In the Place of the Public Sphere?*, Berlin: oe + b books, 2005.

10 Bernardo Secchi provides an extremely important and effective description of public space in Siena in his *La città del ventesimo secolo*, Rome-Bari: Laterza, 2006, pp. 54–62.

11 With specific reference to Alison and Peter Smithson's definition of *Cluster*.

12 F. Haydn, R. Temel (ed. by), *Temporary Urban Spaces*, Basel, Birkhauser: 2006.

13 According to Nils Norman, the cities become cleaner and safer, design gets more abundant and paranoid, the arousal of fear guides the design of urban fixtures more than function (N. Norman, "Urbanomics", in S. Sheikh, op. cit., p. 36).

14 Z. Bauman, *Modus vivendi. Inferno e utopia del mondo liquido*, Rome-Bari: Laterza, 2007, p. 105 (translation by Robert Burns).

Mecanoo architects   **Montevideo**

2003–05
Rotterdam,
The Netherlands

Montevideo consists of a composition of intersecting volumes, part of which is suspended above the pier. The building refers to the interbellum high-rise buildings of New York, Chicago and Boston: brick built, with refined detailing and use of colour, a lot of roof terraces and loggias. The first two floors are built of steel and bear the 152 metres-high tower and the Water Apartments jutting 16 metres out. The 27 floors above are executed with a concrete climbing form. From the 28th floor steel is used, so that the floors of these apartments are freely subdivisible. This allows the building to achieve a very varied spatial structure: 192 dwellings with no less than 54 different types and different floor heights divided amongst Loft, City, Sky and Water apartments. All this on top of a two-storey underground parking facility.

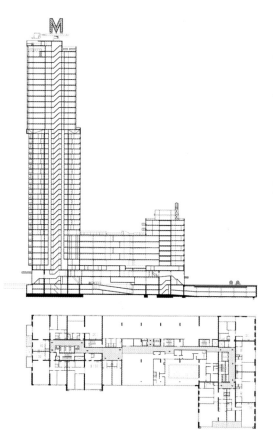

Ábalos & Herreros

The Woermann Tower and Square

2005
Las Palmas de Gran
Canaria, Spain

How would one wish to live on the Istmo, one of the most sensitive places in Las Palmas, a small neck that connects the continuous built mass of the city with the uninhabited peninsula of La Isleta? Ábalos & Herreros imagines houses with generous high ceilings akin to traditional ones, enjoying views like those we might have from a natural observation point, huge expanses protected by long artificial shadows – brise-soleil – and natural ones – plant motifs in the thickness of the glass – so they would never again be lacking. The Woermann Tower is a virtual wood from which to enjoy the utopia of living immersed in a hybrid landscape.

It sets out to embody the illusions, desires and fantasies of a society that seeks to discover a compromise between nature and development, an intense form of life faithful to the landscape: another beauty.

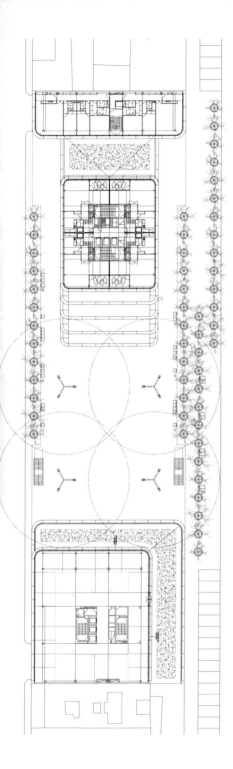

Gigon/Guyer Architekten
Annette Gigon,
Mike Guyer

Broëlberg I

1994–96
Kilchberg, Switzerland

Six sites were selected for the construction of concentrated, volumetrically distinct three-storey buildings with varying concepts of habitation, forming a volumetric complex, linked via a one-storey podium with space for parking underneath. Two of the buildings house four apartments and a penthouse each, the third consists of a row of four units. In most of the apartments, the kitchen and dining areas face the podium, while the living room with projecting conservatory and the bedrooms face the landscape.

Large windows are indicative of the luxurious setting, as they afford a magnificent view of the lake and the surrounding parkland. The dark brown of the outside walls enhances the volumetric appearance of the structure, while evoking plowed fields, tree trunks and anonymous agricultural buildings.

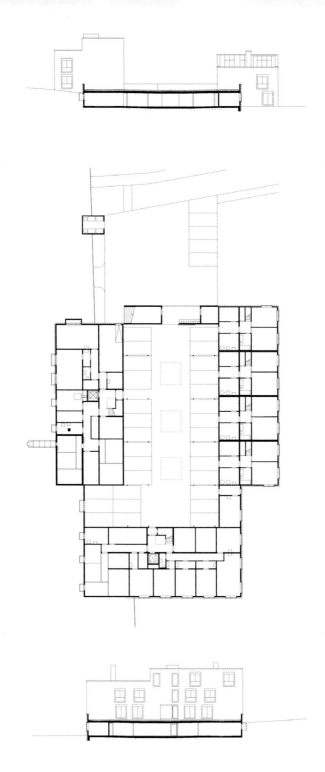

Josep Lluís Mateo   **Sant Jordi Students' Hall of Residence**

2006
Avenida Sarrià-Calle
Ricardo Zamora,
Barcelona, Spain

The new Sant Jordi Students' Hall of Residence has been designed as an urban
feature in its own right, while respecting the logic and coherence of the space
in which it stands. The building is the final piece in a unitary residential urban
development. It consists of a tall volume, the continuation of the existing
residential blocks, and a shorter volume, which is translucent, light and colourful
and which stands in the middle of an empty area, thereby subtly dividing the
public space.
The tall building is a continuous ribbon that folds in such a way that the roof is
built on one of its many pleats. The chromatic development of the building, which
helps to give it the open, vital character typical of a university centre, is the work
of the artist Sílvia Hornig.

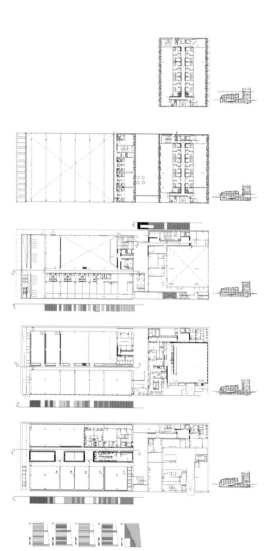

Delugan Meissl
Associated Architects

The Beam

1996
Vienna, Austria

The laconic form as "horizontal high-rise" and the greatly visible location of this apartment complex referred to as the "Beam" signal, at first glance, both its integration in an originally greater overall concept and its individualistic conception. With the Beam, Delugan Meissl succeeds in conceiving a contemporary interpretation of the classical residential building theme. The traditional slab form is revolutionized via ingenious sectional strategies that run from the centre to the edge as well as from the bottom to the top: the 250 apartments extend from front to back, some of them are *maisonnettes* and have both a glazed loggia and a kind of glassed-in vestibule as part of the network of walkways/accessways for entering the apartments along the glazed backs of the building.

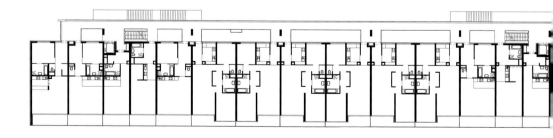

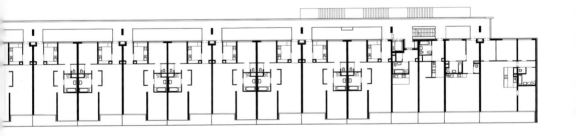

Architectuurstudio
Herman Hertzberger

Rotterdamerstrasse Housing Complex

1997
Düren, Germany

This residential complex consists of some 140 units of various dwelling types and with a shared meeting area, all beneath a roof that doubles as an almost rectangular frame round an open central courtyard.

The continuous roof suggests a perimeter block, yet the units placed beneath it are held clear of one another, leaving openings everywhere that access the inner courtyard on all sides. Again, whereas the central court of a perimeter block would be taken up with individual gardens, here it is pre-eminently a community space with a street running through it and space for parking cars. All entrances to the houses are on this inner side, which has taken over the function of the streets traditionally around the outside of the block. In this zone there is room enough left for playgrounds and for community activities that can be watched from all sides.

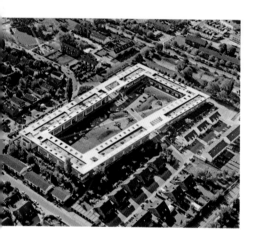

C+S ASSOCIATI
Carlo Cappai,
Maria Alessandra
Segantini

University Student Housing at Novoli

2006
Novoli, Florence, Italy

The 250 university student housing units and associated service areas are laid out on four upper floors. The underground floor is occupied by a parking garage, while the ground floor houses shops and the university cafeteria.

The design of the blocks, the conservation of fixed external borders, the materials, and the system of vertical openings have suggested the theme of "constructed mass", where the contrast between materials takes the form of vibrating shadows against a substantially monochrome background. The external edges of the buildings are marked by the regular spacing of the formworks of the ground floor's bare cement base and the wooden "shingle" shade system that casts light vibrations of shadow.

The distribution system of the student living quarters is arranged around a metal *ballatoio*, or elevated walkway, giving access, with varying degrees of privacy, to the student communal areas.

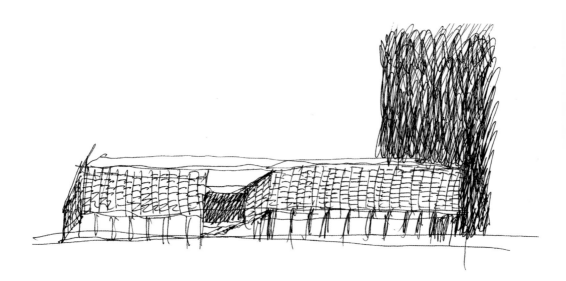

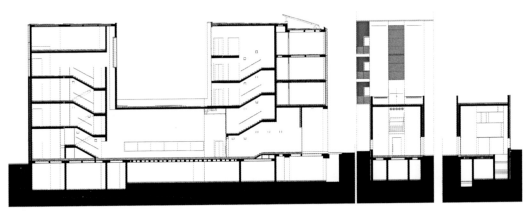

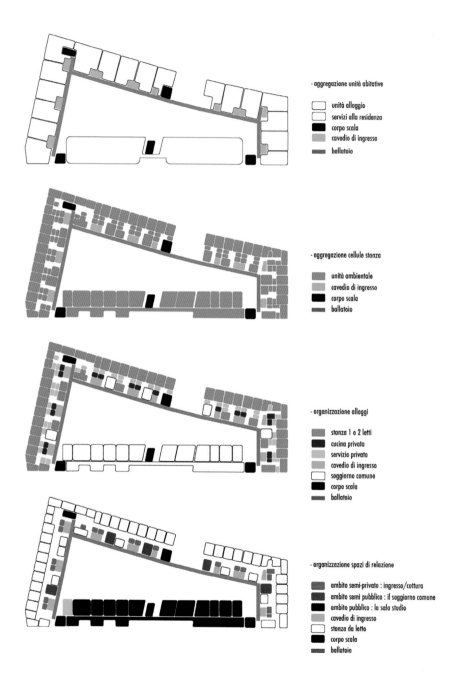

- aggregazione unità abitative

- [ ] unità alloggio
- [ ] servizi alla residenza
- corpo scala
- cavedio di ingresso
- ballatoio

- aggregazione cellule stanza

- unità ambientale
- cavedio di ingresso
- corpo scala
- ballatoio

- organizzazione alloggi

- stanza 1 o 2 letti
- cucina privata
- servizio privato
- cavedio di ingresso
- soggiorno comune
- corpo scala
- ballatoio

- organizzazione spazi di relazione

- ambito semi-privato : ingresso/cottura
- ambito semi pubblico : il soggiorno comune
- ambito pubblico : la sala studio
- cavedio di ingresso
- stanza da letto
- corpo scala
- ballatoio

Steven Holl Architects
Steven Holl, Tim Bade

Simmons Hall

2002
Cambridge,
Massachusetts,
United States

The 350-bed residence is envisioned as part of the city form and campus form
with a concept of "porosity". It is a vertical slice of a city ten stories tall and
116 metres long. House dining is on street level, like a street front restaurant
with a special awning and outdoor tables.

The "sponge" concept transforms a porous building morphology via a series of
programmatic and bio-technical functions. The overall building mass has five large-
scale openings corresponding to main entrances, panoramic corridors, and the
main outdoor activity terraces of the dormitory connected to programmes such as
the gym. The "PerfCon" structure is a unique design, allowing for maximum
flexibility and interaction.

In the deep setting of the numerous windows, colour is applied to the head and
jamb, creating identity for each of the ten "houses" within the overall building.

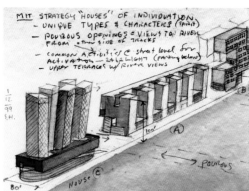

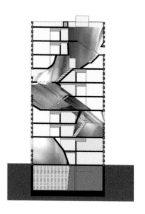

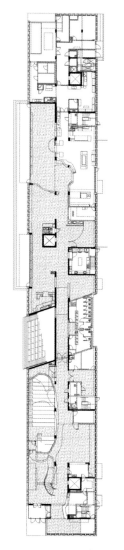

Peter Ebner
Günter Eckerstorfer

Student Housing in Salzburg

1998
Salzburg, Austria

The students' hostel, which is used as a hotel during the summer season,
incorporates business premises and a farmers' market on the ground
level. The financial revenues of the hotel help to reduce the boarding cost
for the students. The diverse needs of the occupants had to be respected,
so that the lifestyle of the young people is not affected by the simplistic style
of a hotel, and this is what gave this project such a broad definition.
The building, facing north towards the square, mirrors the parallel sequence
of the hotel/student rooms in a discrete glass facade, which guarantees sufficient
light in the shadow cast by the mountain. The entrance divides the building into
two sections of different size. The front door portrays a tunnel, which opens
up to a spacious hall, offering a sweeping view of the mountain.

Residential Buildings in Innsbruck

1997
Innsbruck, Austria

In order to lower the rent for the average income, architects as well as developers in Europe are under the pressure of lowering the cost of social housing. On the other hand, cheap "poor man's houses" should be avoided. How to combine these opposing demands is demonstrated by this project on the outskirts of Innsbruck. It not only conserves energy and is inexpensive, but also uses high standards of residential design.

Compact building volumes with relatively small exterior surfaces and highly insulated exterior walls are associated with a not effortless but very efficient environmental control system, combining the following factors: controlled ventilation of the apartments with thermal recovery, hot water provided by solar collectors, using rainwater for flushing toilets. Both units consume about 70% less energy than one conventional residential building.

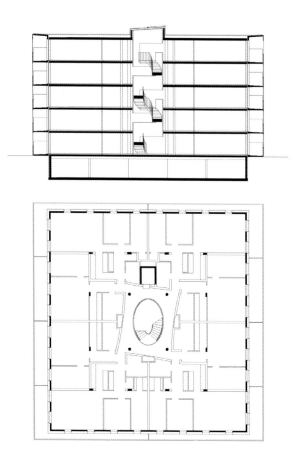

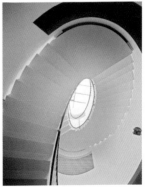

Student Housing in Landrain

2000
Landrain, Germany

The project is composed of eight buildings, two of which are connected together by means of a broad loggia containing the stairway and functioning as a gathering place and access-way to the upper floor.

The facades reinterpret the pre-existing elements in a contemporary key and are characterized by the horizontal trend of the composition: the external skin is made of blue-green U-glass elements over sliding black perforated sheet steel panels that modulate the shade and act as anti-intrusion barriers.

The interior bearing walls are finished exclusively in smoothed lightened aerated concrete, maintaining the same chromatic characteristics as the exterior.

The linoleum floor covering has a blue-green colour and all the furnishings are finished in maple veneer.

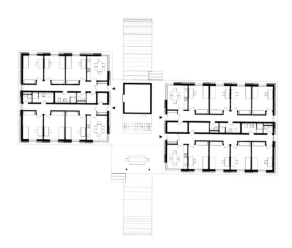

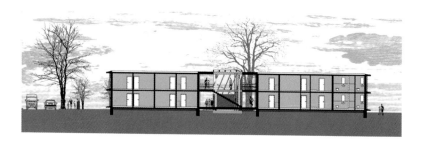

Mecanoo architects

Oeverpad, Amsterdam-Osdorp

2003–05
Amsterdam,
The Netherlands

The brief called for a closed building block four to five stories high. Leaving out the side on the Sloterplas and stacking these apartments on the other three sides means that all 120 apartments have a view of the lake.
The building stands on a transparent plinth of glass and grating, so that it appears almost to float. The basis of the building consists of four stories of raw, orange-brown bricks that suit the natural quality of the surroundings.
The upper floors look lighter because of the use of a lot of glass in which the sky is reflected. The courtyard facades are constructed from vertical wooden slats.
The cool appearance of the perforated steel "curtain" used to clad the access gallery ensures a lively contrast to the warm look of the wooden interior facades.

Breda Carré Building

2000
Breda, The Netherlands

The Carré was designed as a relatively compact block made up of a series
of densely stacked units.
The internal courtyard is planned as a quiet place in the Chassé terrain.
There are 144 apartments and 6 shop units for small businesses in the building.
Unusually, 100 of the apartments are rent controlled, the other 44 were sold
on the open market by the client/developer with considerable success.
The building was carefully designed for retiring baby boomers, people who move
to a smaller house.
Completely clad in wood veneer, the Carré is a friendly brute, which only reveals
its relatively rugged detailing on close inspection. The galleries of the building
are sheltered from the elements by loosely placed glass boards. The structure
of the galleries is made of a robustly detailed galvanized steel framework.
All the apartments have balconies with custom-designed (and made) sun shading
elements in expanded aluminium sheet, framed in aluminium profiles.

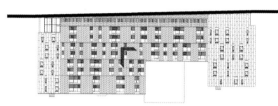

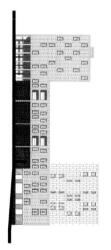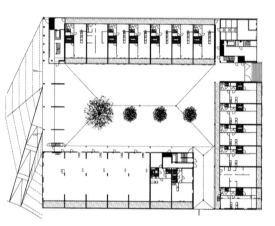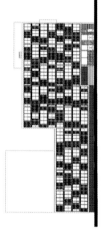

Birkimörk Halfway House

2006–07
Hveragerði, Iceland

The apartment housing is located in a town of about 1,700 inhabitants that lies some 45 km east of Reykjavik. Surrounded by an eminent mountain range to the north, the town is conveniently located on the Ring Road, Iceland's most important highway.

PK Arkitektar was commissioned to plan a facility for severely handicapped youngsters in Hveragerði. From the beginning it was clear to the architects that the task was to create a home rather than simply an institution.

The architectural appearance is simple and characterized by a sincere and clear composition of two white blocks with different heights and separated by a distribution corridor. The apartments area and functional spaces are connected by a corridor in the middle of the building which brings daylight in, providing a warm and serene ambience.

The five apartments are fully equipped for severely handicapped youngsters. They measure 34.5 sq.m each, with their own kitchens and bathrooms.

Urban Redevelopment Programme, Housing Towers

2005
Milan, Italy

The towers are part of an urban redevelopment programme implemented by the City of Milan for the revival of a former industrial area in Via Pompeo Leoni, known as the "OM" zone. The choice of tower format ensures a view of the surrounding landscape and visibility for the project itself. The buildings are strongly characterized and the variety of apartment types, different on every floor, creates differentiation and autonomy on the facades. These are faced in *pietra dorata* and slate. The former is a light, rough-cut honey coloured sandstone; the latter is split and used on the windowed sections of the facade corresponding to the sleeping quarters, thus creating a strong colour contrast between the slate and the glass.

Different apartment types give the building high flexibility in meeting a diversity of contemporary living needs. They range from studio apartments for singles to three-bedroom units for large families, and all contemplate space requirements for home offices and future expectations for a generalized use of the global information network.

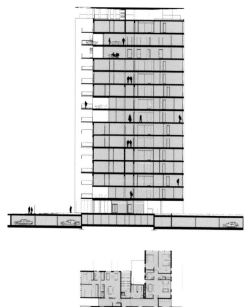

Sustainability

Sustainable Housing
Benno Albrecht

The debate on the design of low-cost housing was forgotten for a long time, sidelined by recent interest in the ephemeral world of architectural fashion. However, in this period of oblivion, residential construction was the favoured area of research on the frontiers of sustainability, something that was always treated with contempt by the star system and its exponents. This has happened because it was precisely in the field of residential architecture that it was possible to experiment with new techniques and technologies, even on small-scale projects. Today, a new civic awareness encompassing the importance of collective responsibility for climate change together with the commercial potential and appeal of "sustainable architecture" have brought residential architecture, including affordable housing, back into vogue. And this architecture is now seen through the lens of the potential offered by the science of sustainability.

This is edifying for those who are directly involved in the search for new housing standards and a reduction in resource use, including human, natural and physical resources. For us, architecture has assumed (or reassumed) a new fundamental ethical value and has become responsible for the new fiduciary relationship between human action and the natural environment.

But once again we find the publicist lagging behind the most advanced research.

We have realized that the most effective response to correct the distortions produced by scientific-technological-industrial culture in its transformation of our territory is not just increasing the efficiency of a single building component, but rethinking the entire current urban structure. Even the best performing building – zero emissions and zero consumption – has no value if it is incorporated into a non-sustainable, degraded and unattractive urban fabric. What is necessary is a shift in scale and a change in mental attitude.

We have to think of the city as an integrated system of developments, each with its own centre. It is thus a multicentric system (where the centres contain the main transport nodes and urban facilities), or a multipolar system, deemphasizing the word "centre", which evokes the idea of historically evolving settlements and high-density housing with clear boundaries between the urban fabric and the open spaces of the surrounding countryside. The reorganized scheme calls for compact units and close-knit urban nuclei containing a functional mix that encourages different forms and levels of sociality.

The post-war city plan can undergo a metamorphosis. Post-war development has to undergo profound changes regarding both undeveloped and developed spaces. The contemporary city was not planned and constructed in adherence to rules whose goal was to produce satisfying residential systems and environments. It no longer has spaces into which it can expand, but it has many that it can redevelop, such as those on the peripheral, marginal, fringe areas. They are cities that are not cities, too built-up to be a non-urban landscape and not built-up enough to be a bona fide urban centre. A policy of densification of post-war development is necessary.

It is thus opportune to propose new and more effective development densities that are adjusted to suit the local urban context and typological characteristics. Promoting *a densification and a redistribution of urban developments*, beyond merely encouraging an intensification of activities, also allows public services, such as transport, to become efficient while allowing high environmental quality to be maintained (including appropriate standards of privacy, minimum necessary personal spaces and maximum noise and pollution abatement measures).

Incentives should be provided for the intermingling of multiple activities (multiple uses of time and spaces) and not their segregation into homogeneous, monofunctional zones, assuming as the unit of measurement the distances that can be travelled on foot. It is necessary to promote mixed land uses to favour nearness between the different venues of daily life (home, workplace, services, recreation areas and green areas), ensuring maximum efficiency of public infrastructure and services use and guaranteeing safety and security in the use of public spaces.

We have to promote and support new projects for affordable housing that reduce costs across the board (social costs, construction costs, building lifecycle costs), requiring that a proportion of development plans (including those not directed to a specific sector) be dedicated to affordable housing, offer mixed use and be set up in such a way that different income groups and socioeconomic classes can live near one another – as reflected in the horizontal stratification of historical cities – in order to favour greater cohesion among different social groups, thus reducing the phenomenon of ghettoization.[1]

The design of climatic architecture also has to be incentivized. We are convinced that incorporating climate factors into the interpretation of a context and placing architectural and urban design strategies within a broader overall strategy of reduction in resource (natural, physical and human) consumption and waste will lead to the creation of a new reference system that in turn will lead to, or will be capable of leading to, different design solutions. We must design with the objective of zero resource consumption and zero emissions.

Within this framework, implementing high quality pro-sustainability architecture with cutting-edge building techniques, i.e., using building materials appropriately and seeking to use recyclable materials and sustainable technologies as much as possible, becomes an obvious and obligatory choice.

It is a question of setting up a sustainable urban design project that allows us to reduce carbon emissions to zero and that will continue to be viable over a broadly range of changing climatic conditions.

We can seek an urban architecture with the fundamental value of a high capacity to adapt to transformations in environmental setting. The sincere and proactive approach of architectural culture has to act not on the exterior forms, but on the inner structures that determine the forms.

We are ready for new and audacious challenges.

Quoting a famous declaration by Winston Churchill,[2] we too may say: "We shall not fail or falter; we shall not weaken or tire... Give us the tools and we will finish the job."

[1] One of the most recent contributions to the debate, which had seemed to have run itself out, regards housing design and resident needs. See G. Turchini, M. Grecchi, *Nuovi modelli per l'abitare. L'evoluzione edilizia residenziale di fronte alle nuove esigenze*, Milan: Il Sole 24 Ore SpA, 2006.

[2] Speech before the Joint Session of the US Congress in Washington on December 26, 1941, requesting the intervention of the United States in World War II.

Lohbach Residential Project

1998
Innsbruck, Austria

Economically and ecologically optimized residential construction was required here. Thus the decision to build cube-like structures with interior access and a projecting balcony zone that can be closed off from the outside with copper sun-protecting elements. The open spaces – including small gardens in front of the ground level apartments – make it easy to forget the density of construction. Hence the copper cubes envisioned by the architects are really there and the only openings are those created by residents who have their shutters open. This interplay between (primarily) closed and (partly) opened surfaces is extremely appealing.
All the ecological possibilities allowed by today's technology were applied to these houses. These include solar energy panels and heat recovery plants.

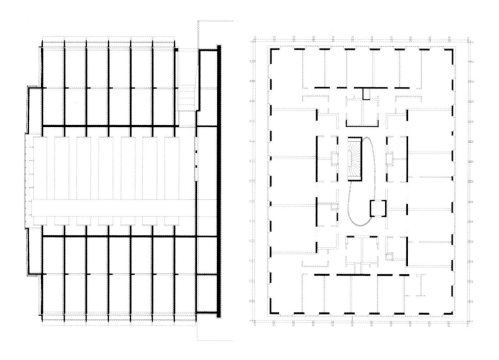

Baumschlager-Eberle **BTV Commercial and Residential Building**

1997
Wolfurt, Austria

This place is characterized today by large but modest buildings, between which older buildings have been encapsulated.

The front part of the building, oriented to the public, is occupied by the facilities of the bank, whereas the back part, oriented to the garden, contains apartments of different size and patterns.

The larch wood lattice works as a memorable sign, with its horizontally moving elements, which wrap consequently around the glass cube. The lattice serves not only the purpose of protection from sun and sight, but also lends the building a large degree of homogeneity. The flexible moving elements yield a simultaneously multilayered and attractive image of the facade. The wood lattice originates the changing play of light and shadow and thus shapes the interior spaces as well, especially the multifunctional hall on the fourth floor.

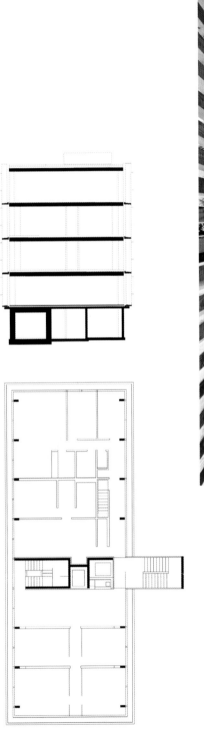

Delugan Meissl
Associated Architects

Kallco Projekt 7.14

1999
Vienna, Austria

The Town House Wimbergergasse occupies a building gap that arose
in the dense urban grid of Gründerzeit buildings. Its mixed use as office and
apartment complex fits quite well into the structure of the seventh district,
which, as a residential neighbourhood, traditionally exhibits a high density
of smaller businesses.
The design shows Delugan Meissl's two dominant design motifs: the
accentuation of topography and the space-containing feature of the facade.
What emerges is a strictly composed grid that comes from the pattern produced
by the different levels of the apartments and staircases in the background,
along with the rhythmic divisions of the glazed front. Together they make a very
strong visual impact.

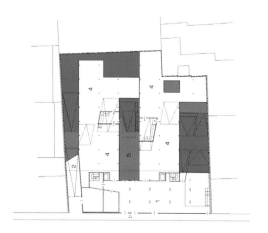

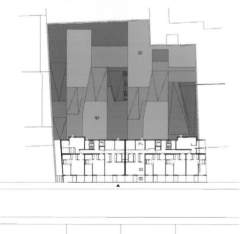

3X Nielsen Architects   **Sustained Ecohousing**

1998
Bramdrupdam, Kolding,
Denmark

This project, first prize in a competition for sustained ecological housing, focuses on solar walls, surface limitations and use of the terrain. Heated air from the solar wall panels is directed into the heavy apartment sections of concrete, which function as heat storage. The heat is slowly liberated again during nighttime, and this effect reduces energy consumption remarkably. Other ecological aspects are the re-use of surface water in the common laundries and a central garbage sorting. The housing project is built on a square sited in an open green landscape near Kolding, Jutland. Fifty-four dwellings are concentrated into a kibbutz-like experience of narrow paths with sudden openings towards the vast landscape. Inside the houses the main focus has been to give the tenants a high-quality experience of space.

Holz Box Tirol,
Erich Strolz

Terraced Housing

1999
Innsbruck, Austria

The land under the Innsbruck Nordkette slopes off in two directions. The plot is about 1,000 sq.m wide, the upper strip of which town planners had intended to use as an access way and parking facilities. The graded tower and terrace houses for a private building company debunk two preconceptions: first, that "prefab wooden boxes with low-energy values" inevitably result in spatial schematism; and second, that architecture destroys the local slopes' topography. The project meets the following criteria: a maximum of natural area preservation, the least possible interference by the houses with the lay of the land, roofed parking along the road without the common shelter-like housing altogether offsetting the contrast between densification and exposition to the valley view, between optimizing external exposure and ensuring privacy.

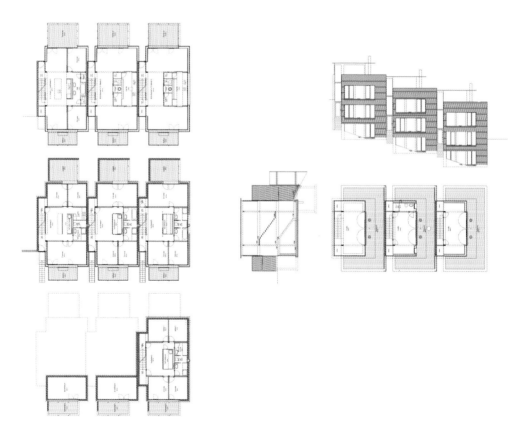

Metrogramma
Andrea Boschetti,
Alberto Francini

Domus Malles

2006–07
Bolzano, Italy

Domus Malles is a building of high architectural quality that focuses on the comfort of low-cost dwellings representing the principles of eco-sustainability to the point that they have earned "B-type indoor climate" certification. One of the main characteristics of this complex entails dwelling spaces that are always different from one another, thus ensuring a broad range of options. The fourteen apartments reflect three different types: apartments with gardens on the ground floor; apartments with a terrace or loggia on the first, second and third floors; and attic apartments with hanging gardens on the fourth floor. The heterogeneity of the elevations and their accuracy of detail highlight the conceptual variety within, the result being a contemporary building that integrates harmoniously into the pre-existing urban context.

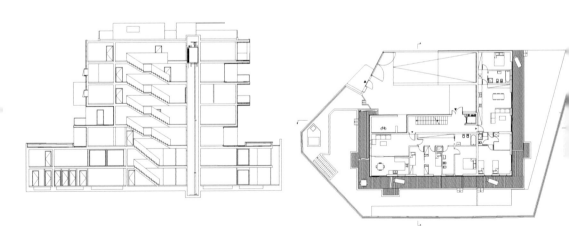

Benno Albrecht
with Fabio Mensi

13 Low-cost Dwellings

2006
Palazzolo sull'Oglio,
Brescia, Italy

The 13 low-cost dwellings (750 euros/sq.m) were built in accordance with the Low-Cost Popular Housing Plan (*Piano per l'Edilizia Economica Popolare* – PEEP), where cost savings is a basic requisite in planning and design and in the awarding of contracts. However, excellent quality materials and sophisticated technical systems are used in constructing the dwellings, in line with sustainable architecture criteria.

The dwellings use an outfitted wall containing the chimneys for natural ventilation, cooling and dehumidification. The central courtyard is insulated using recycled paper.

The building was made using traditional methods of concrete, double-walled partitions and walls in soft-paste solid bricks buttressed by pilaster strips that contain all ascending and descending building utility systems, resulting in the possibility of very simple dwellings without need for crawl spaces for utility systems, while also simplifying the construction and maintenance processes.

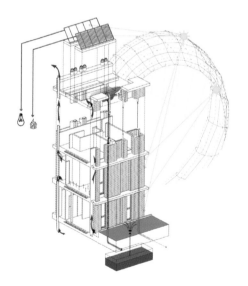
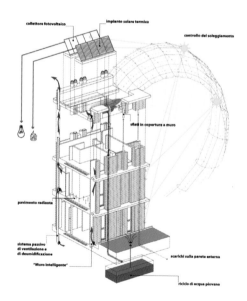

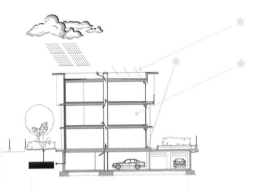

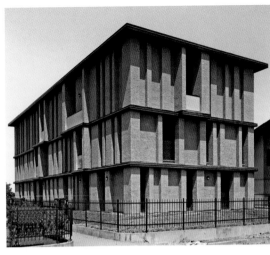

Georg W. Reinberg   **Rappersberg**

1999–2001
Burgerland, Neusiedler
See, Austria

The aims of the project were: living closer to the natural environment and the water; building with wood and achieving a low energy consumption; prefabrication; active and passive use of solar energy; ecological building; natural cooling in summer.

The buildings – single houses and terrace houses – occupy an area realized with an homogeneous constructive concept: a central wall and a platform forming a "massive core". This "core" can give back the stored heat of winter sun or the summer night's cool and it is formed with prefabricated elements with high thermal insulation. On this load-bearing structure stands the wooden roof; the great overhang protects the south front from the summer solar radiation and, in the meantime, allows the complete exposure to the sun during the winter.

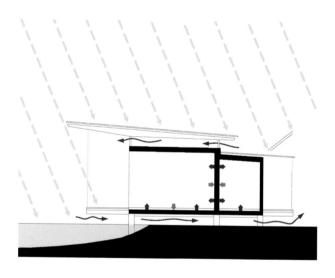

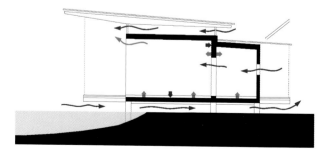

Transforming

Flexibility and the Architectural Project
Camillo Botticini

The concept of flexibility acquired centrality in the architectural debate start-ing with the criticism of Modernism after World War II. The discussion focussed on the perception that architecture was excessively determining in its spatial arrangements and that this did not allow for subsequent changes that might be seen as being necessary. The potentialities offered by Le Corbusier's *plan libre* appeared to crystallize an idea of habitation that was incapable of con-templating change.

The debate went on, oscillating between the search for a neutral, albeit tech-nologically sophisticated, indeterminacy, which was radicalized in the high tech approach, and that of realizing a form capable of embracing this indetermi-nacy, starting with the stabilization of characteristic traits.

It was in 1960s Italy that Vittorio Gregotti recognized that the form-use-meaning connection called for a relation between the stable characteristics of architecture and those that were modifiable, underlining the need for coher-ence among architectonic components.[1] In this sense, research into building types could also be interpreted as an exploration of the relationship between the *permanent* and the *variable* characteristics of architecture. The attempt was to work out the relationships between permanent structures in the inhabited space (whose value would no longer be a question of chance, but the expres-sion of the conformational potentialities of the typological architectonic space) and the varying conditions of inhabitation, which were an expression of the rap-id and incessant flow of social, economic and cultural change. Even though the question in this case regards more the relation between memory, permanence of archetypes and their generative-adaptive capabilities, forcing an interpreta-tion of the nature of the building type as it has been configured, the flexibili-ty and adaptive capacity of the inhabited system ends up directly correlated with the presence of permanent structures that are capable of metabolizing vari-ations.[2] In this sense, we may discern a neo-functionalist version, open to change, of a debate whose limit and value have been to turn every act of rea-soning to a rethinking of architecture vis-à-vis the architectural tradition and historical urban structures.

Regarding the urban dimension, starting in the 1960s, the debate encom-passed criticism of the excessive determination of spaces and their codifica-tion also on the territorial scale, which was seen as an expression of function-alist urban planning. By imposing physical categories, this planning assigned a place to every function, limiting the diversity of spatial uses,[3] thwarting the multifunctionality, complexity and flexibility of urban arrangements.

Today this criticism has been substantially overcome by the real condition of what has been called the "post-modern city",[4] indeterminate playgrounds, and we now witness the materialization of development that obliterates iden-tity without producing alternatives endowed with qualities. The world we all know was created, where the public spaces are segregated and sequestered, and disappear. Open space becomes progressively marginalized as scrap and the his-toric nuclei are reduced to shopping and service districts.

The apparent flexibility turns out to be – without any prospect in the development for an idea of transformation – the result of urban and architectural development that not only *neutralizes* the existing space, but is also devoid of identity and meaningful differences.

What emerges is that the issue of flexibility profoundly determines the very meaning and nature of architecture on all scales. The concept, understood in its broadest and most general sense, may be taken as the "capacity for adaptation expressed in the ability to suggest a possible transformation". The relationship determined by change in the spatial-temporal dimension is brought into the picture together with the use and meaning that derives from it.

If the architecture changes, how can we follow the change and verify the final form?

If we investigate specific architectures and verify their spatial variability, we may be able to identify an abstract conceptualization that allows us to interpret flexibility via the role it plays as an element in the project.

The initial categorization of flexibility as *specific spatial* thing (that is, implicated in the project, which, while maintaining its own identity, accepts fixed elements that allow variable uses) finds an emblematic expression in the work of Louis Kahn. It is in the separation between "served" and "serving" spaces that the order imposed on space creates stable nuclei that allow flexibility in the determination of the served, inhabited spaces, which are freed from accessory spaces, whether technical or functional.

Projects such as the Richards Laboratories in Philadelphia, where the utility systems find a specific and emblematic placement in the towers adjacent to the inhabited floors, or the Salk Laboratories in La Jolla, California, where floors dedicated to research alternate with technical, utility levels, show how, in types that may be considered extreme for their highly specific use, flexibility implies principles such as those of accessory or utility spaces alongside but distinct from the human-use spaces, which thus remain free of hindrances and constraints.

In this sense, Kahn's lesson introduces a central aspect: flexibility demands stable nuclei in order to determine itself. The complexity of the project lies in identifying *how* and *what* these nuclei have to be.

We must also point out that Kahn's architecture touches on another principle, that of flexibility as *neutral space*, which is made possible by construction technology capable of erecting great spans that render the enclosed space wholly available. Examples range from Buckminster Fuller's geodesic structures to Mies van der Rohe's Convention Hall and Vilanova Artigas's projects for the university of São Paulo.

It is in the myth of neutrality, of an unlimited expanse of roofs with a minimal number of support points, of suspended structures or structures that integrate the utility components into themselves in machinelike perfection, that the high tech parabola is resolved. It finds its principle exemplars in large-scale infrastructures such as airports or train stations, among which we cite London's Stansted airport by Norman Foster, where the structure is composed of a system of steel umbrellas like a repeating Meccano construction or a nineteenth-century market, offering a freely usable and extendable space. The limitation of this approach, which is frequently atopic, neutral and impositional with regard to the context, does not entirely cancel out its potential.

Another categorization sees flexibility as being *temporal*, both in the synchronous sense, as a change that allows reversible variations in arrangement and use, and in the diachronic sense, in an architecture that includes design for its own change. This sort of flexible architecture *voluntarily* modifies itself, providing a different and reversible use. Emblematic in this regard are projects such as Wiel Arets's mobile football pitch in Holland, which becomes the roof for a public space and a playing ground, or Jean Prouvé's project in Clichy, a market in the morning and a theatre in the evening.

This interpretation, coinciding with spatial variability, highlights the complexity of the theme. It is in residential architecture that some very interesting results have been achieved, as in the distributive adaptability of Gerrit Rietveld's Schröder House, where sliding walls allow different uses of the interior space during the day depending on the needs of the inhabitants, or Steven Holl's houses in Fukuoka, where we witness the idea of a possible modification of interior space by means of walls that can revolve or shift position.[5]

Another flexibility mode is *diachronic*, associated with the ability of a building to undergo interior changes for a possible future use, providing for easy substitution of components, modifications or additions, a work that is open to a future that cannot always be foreseen.

If the prototype for this mode can be found in a rationalist project, such as Cesare Cattaneo's House for a Christian family, which entailed a dwelling-place that could adapt to changing needs associated with population growth (which at the time was much stronger than it is today), experiments in this genre have also been undertaken in more recent housing projects: the projects of MVRDV and Rem Koolhas in Holland, the experimental projects of Mansilla + Tuñón in Spain or of Helena Nijric in Croatia and Álvaro Siza's famous neighbourhood project in Evora, as well as the dwellings designed by Alejandro Aravena in Chile.

Flexibility may thus be defined by evaluating the centrality of the spatial-temporal dimension, preventing form and programme from coinciding with one another in the project, anticipating and allowing different and even antithetical uses, and incorporating such principles into the project as the possibility of disassembly, adaptation, addition and change. Hence flexibility may be condensed into the dialectical coupling of the permanence or variability of characteristics, the stability of that which cannot change and that which can be re-determined.

Today, flexibility has also come to mean adaptability in orienting oneself toward an ever-increasing specificity of and attention to the components of inhabitability, such as climate control, acoustics and durability of components, and in designing spatial structures which, abandoning the myth of neutrality, are stable and recognizable yet genetically capable of embracing change.

[1] V. Gregotti, *Il territorio dell'architettura*, Milan: Feltrinelli, 2008.
[2] C. M. Aris, *Le variazioni dell'identità*, Milan: Clup, 1990.
[3] H. Lefebvre, *La produzione dello spazio*, Milan: Moizzi Editore, 1974.
[4] G. Amendola, *La città postmoderna*, Bari: Laterza, 2000.
[5] S. Holl, *Parallax*, Princeton (NJ): Princeton University Press, 1998.

Kazuyo Sejima
& Associates

Gifu Kitagata Apartments

1998–2000
Kitagata, Motosu-gun,
Gifu Prefecture, Tokyo,
Japan

The project, under the direction of Atelier Isozaki, is part of a larger project to build 430 residential units, of which 107 nine-floor units were designed by Sejima. The variable family-type units are freely composed into sections, creating different architectural types, each one with three different access systems. The units are composed of a terrace, a dining room, a bedroom and a typical Japanese room floored in tatami mats. All interior spaces are efficiently arranged to receive the greatest insolation possible. Privacy is achieved by arrangement rather than by separation: the variety of section types allows sleeping and living quarters to be brought together, without that arrangement being perceptible from the outside. Each unit is separated from the front by an intermediate space, an *engawa*, a filter between interior and exterior.

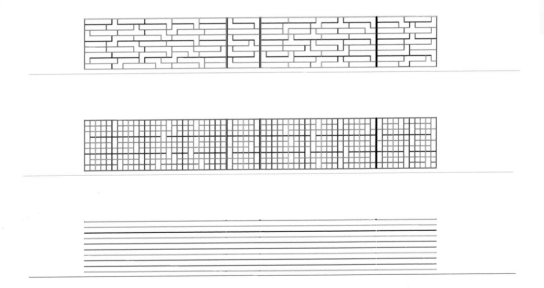

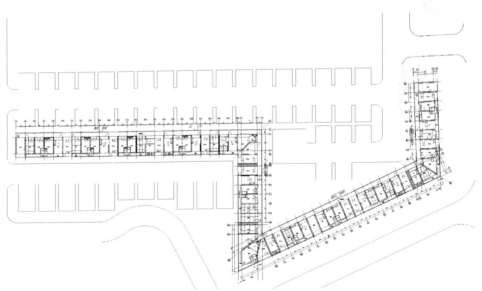

Wolfram Popp
Planungen Architekt
BDA

Estrade-House in Choriner Strasse 56

2001
Berlin, Germany

Popp Planungen built the seven-storey Estrade-House with its own development company.
Each of the two apartments per floor consists of a main area and a service zone which runs the full depth of the unit. The two are so sensitively correlated that the whole is a successful combination of spaciousness, comfort and privacy. Wolfram Popp does not build closed rooms, but rather areas whose borders remain open and alterable, thereby offering a variety of options for use.
Two elements determine these relations. First, there are the *estrades*, which are elevated platforms running along the entire width of the apartment, at front and rear. The second element is the "gill-wall", consisting of twelve wooden ceiling-high panels that run on two tracks above and one below, and can thus be slid as well as rotated.

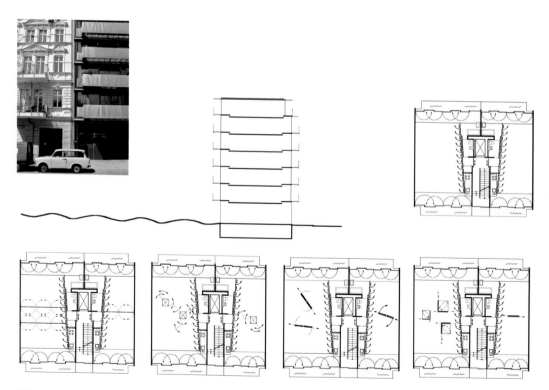

Water Villas

2001
Almere,
The Netherlands

The 48 water villas are situated in an experimentally developed housing area at the periphery of Almere. The concept for the water villas was about creating a living environment with a maximal flexibility to meet individual needs. Each villa consists of a basic package, which can be extended and elaborated depending on the personal preferences and lifestyle of the client. The basic package consists of two concrete modules of 6 metres in width, 10 metres in depth and 3 metres in height. The first floor is shifted to obtain a roof balcony. An optional package is developed to extend the basic housing type according to individual needs. It offers the possibility to elaborate and increase its volumetric potential.

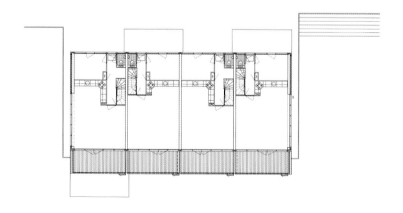

Vondelpark, City Dwelling and Yard Apartments

2000–02
Utrecht,
The Netherlands

The plan consists of a number of zones, each with its own character. The front of the houses is made from fantastically formed brown-reddish bricks, from which zinc covered windows project. The Green Yard forms the second zone. For this sheltered inner area, two closed building blocks are designed. The third zone, the Achterhuizen, is composed of three apartment blocks with 81 Park Apartments. These form simultaneously a gradual transition to the high building blocks of the Voorhuizen and to the lower buildings in the Green Yard.
The Vondelpark is turned into a green, urban living area with a very diverse range of dwellings and thought-out borders of ownership. A public and semi-public area is situated between the different zones, crossed by four paths. By the changing of decoration and use, the public or semi-public character is stressed.

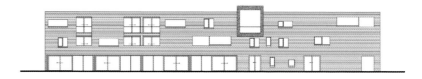

Josep Lluís Mateo   **26 Housing Units in the Borneo Dock**

2000
Amsterdam,
The Netherlands

The project is sited in an unusual situation at the tip of the land surrounded by water on three sides. It is a low mass with projections and recesses. Functionally speaking, the apartments form a huge collective space that invades the terrain. Light penetrates from between the interstices that the protruding volumes leave down towards the ground floor.

The complex is fashioned along the two coordinating axes X, the strict system of parallel concrete walls and same-size windows, and Y: the emergent volumes that move in a non-mechanical way above these. On top of the hard logic of the walls sustaining the building, the facades are fine skins of varying thickness and permeability, and made of tropical wood with a hermetically sealed look handled according to the technologies typical of boat building.

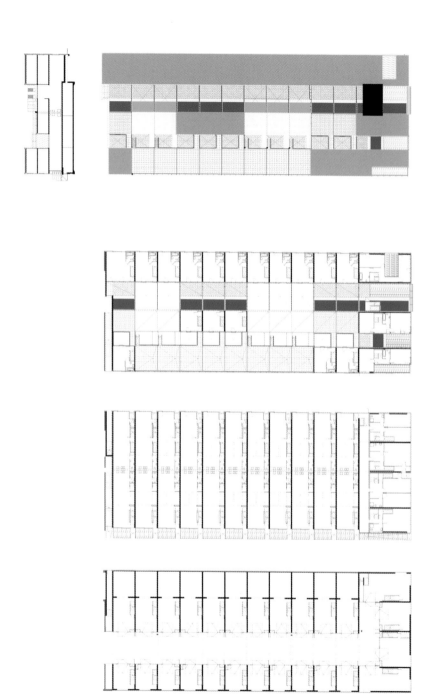

Alejandro Aravena

Quinta Monroy Social Housing

2004
Iquique, Chile

In 2003, the Chile-Barrio Program asked Elemental to develop a design for Quinta Monroy, the last informal settlement in Iquique, a city in the desert. The task was to provide a housing solution to settle the hundred families that illegally occupied a 5,000 sq.m site in the core of Iquique's downtown. Elemental's final proposal was, for the house: a 9 x 9 metre lot with a 6 x 6 x 2.5 metre first stage built unit, containing a bathroom, a kitchen and a loft space. On top of that and over a concrete slab (which we called a horizontal partition wall) we proposed a 6 x 6 x 5 metre duplex apartment with a 3 x 6 x 5 metre initial stage volume containing also a kitchen, a bathroom and a double-height loft space. All of them with individual direct access to the collective space.

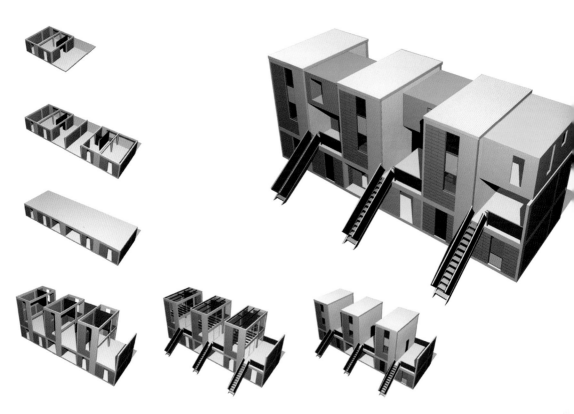

Claus en Kaan
Architecten

Flats for Students UvA-Dek

2001
Amsterdam,
The Netherlands

The building with sixty-one student flats and commercial premises in Amsterdam
is part of a new street frontage. The new wall is made up of three sections.
The corner was designed by Pi De Bruyn, the middle section by VMX Architects
and the longest part by Claus en Kaan. Their original proposal envisaged a
mediation with the neighbouring development built by Hendrik Petrus Berlage
in 1908.
The reinstatement of the street frontage can be seen as a form of urban repair,
albeit without sentimentality or nostalgia. The staggered windows, which break
out of the grid, are a subtle, twenty-first-century variation on the decorative motifs
on windows, doors, bays and cornices characteristic of Dutch architecture
at the time when Sarphatistraat was developed.

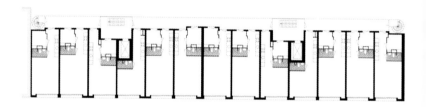

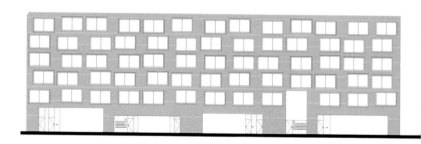

151

153 t/m 157

The Boiler-House Model

2000–01
Almere,
The Netherlands

As we understood it, the assignment required a great degree of flexibility within a clear urban and architectural framework. A standardized core with all provisions is a programmatically, spatially, and financially structured element. In between these cores are large halls: spacious flexible volumes, varying in length, width and height. The hall can be used as a huge loft or divided into a couple of rooms. You can also decide not to build the hall and to place a camper next to the core so that every now and then you can go and camp in the wild.

Standardizing and flexibility are reflected into the materials used. The core, containing the facilities, is clad with African slates representing permanence and sustainability. The flexible halls have aluminium shutters, which stand for changeability and lightness.

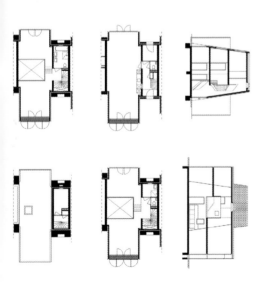

2000–03
Col. Condesa, Mexico
City, Mexico

The south orientation suggested creating an interior patio facing north to accomodate service spaces. Starting from this ground area, the different floor plans are crossed with voids that run from the streets to the interior patio, responding, in each level, to different situations. In this way houses can be identified as distinct units, reflecting the individuality of their dwellers.
To separate the apartments from the street, they are grouped on the fifth to the second level: in the first level, the different apartment services are concentrated in the upper level of the furniture store; the ground floor is used for parking, main entrance and access to the store.

2001–02
Nerima, Tokyo, Japan

This is a collective house with shops standing at the intersection near a suburban station in Tokyo. We treated the style of the openings and the ceiling heights differently according to the function of house and shop. The client's bookstore occupies the ground floors, the rental apartments the upper floors, and the top floor is the client's own house. The bottom of the facade consists of a glass curtain wall, the upper part is made of concrete panels with standard windows. This district's regulations require the building to be set back 1 metre from the road boundary to the height of 6 metres. Therefore, we made the glass curtain wall incline at mid point.

The dwelling units are composed by the pentagonal outline with a square at the centre containing a bathroom and wardrobe to give circulation around the perimeter of the building.

 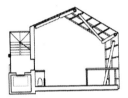 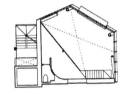

Claus en Kaan
Architecten

Silverline Tower

2000
Almere,
The Netherlands

The tower block containing fifty-eight apartments stands just outside Almere's town centre which, two decades after its construction, is undergoing a major transformation orchestrated by OMA. The tower is on the edge of the planning area, directly overlooking Weerwater, the artificial lake at the heart of this sprawling, polynuclear polder town.

The building has been conceived as a Dutch version of Schiporeit-Heinrich's Lake Point Tower of 1968, an autonomous object standing on the boundary of Chicago and Lake Michigan. The meander form of the tower reinforces the logo-like singularity of this building while at the same time catering to the practical demands of the market: there are plenty of takers for the top and bottom levels of a tower, far fewer for the middle section. The middle has therefore been reduced to a minimum and the top and foot maximized.

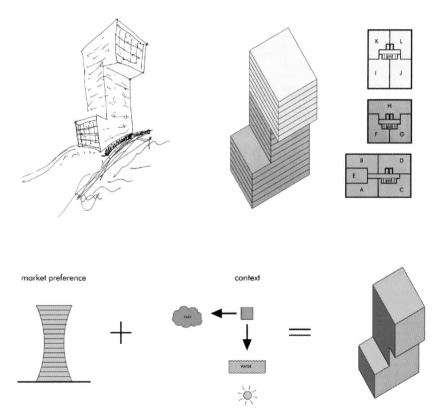

market preference   context

64 Dwellings for Carabanchel Enlargement Plan

2004
Madrid, Spain

In the architecture proposed by Aranguren+Gallegos, the image of the buildings is that of solid volumes sliding across each other. These define a horizontal movement of some over others, all with rows of windows and with different closure systems. Skeleton construction is the most appropriate system. It makes rationalized building methods possible and, at the same time, internal divisions without obstacles. If, due to their installations, kitchens and bathrooms are fixed cores, the rest of the space can be divided by means of movable walls. As a function of daytime and night-time, the house will vary, it will be transformed. In the period of maximum activity, during the daytime, walls will be closer together and beds will be hidden in niches under cupboards and the passages in the central backbone. At night, the space will once more be divided into compartments, with rooms and beds appearing for the resting period. The kitchen is spacious and it is possible to connect it to the living room, since it is considered to be a valued element in new domestic habits. Likewise, a closed and perfectly ventilated space is proposed for the area where clothes are hung to dry. Aranguren+Gallegos believe that this "ambitious" project of raised passages and moveable walls is not at all bad but perhaps too possibilistic since, at practically the same cost, the dwelling gains in more possibilities for use, as a greater surface area of the house can be enjoyed as a single space for multiple activities (work, games, gymnasium, parties...).

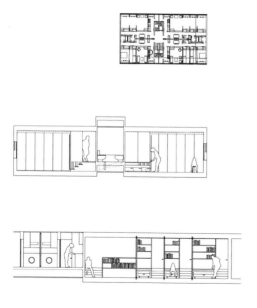

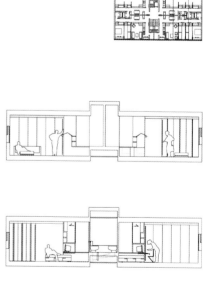

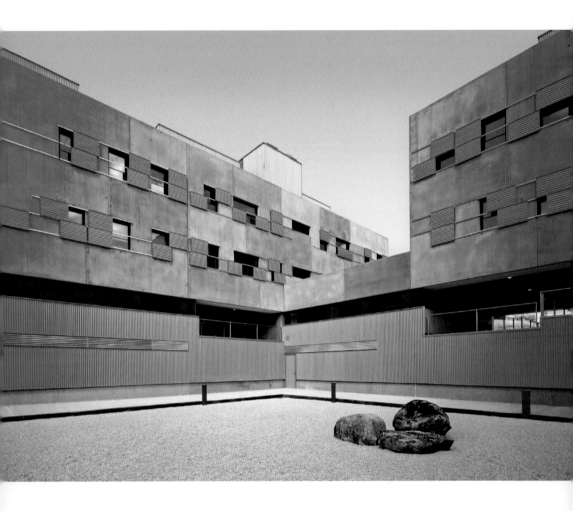

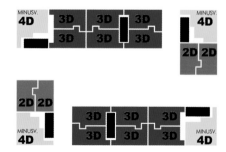

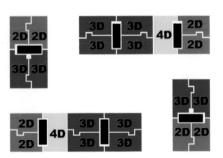

Developing

Dwelling-Context
Carlo Magnani with Andrea Groppello

Everyone says
that it exists
Precisely where,
none can say

In its obstinate duration as a discipline in its own right, architecture has encountered words that have accompanied it along its journey – travelling companions, as it were. These words have historicized architecture, rooting its characteristics in specific periods. The word "context" may be cited as a member of this group. Germinating within an oppositional, critical stance during a certain historical phase, these words assume the task of illuminating new opportunities and possible interpretations for architectural practice, mapping out new territories and establishing new units of measurement.

In Italian dictionaries, the term *contesto* evokes the notion of a situation and a system of relations giving rise to an exchange and intermixing of meanings, whether it is applied to the field of linguistics or to forms of expression in general. In reference to the field of architecture, the notion is a central theme behind a set of experiments embodying a critical stance with respect to an earlier phase of the practice, whose most meaningful paradigm was bound to a linear view of time, a sort of necessary secularization of principles that are substantially abstract. Of course, nothing can be fit perfectly into a representational scheme, nor do newly emerging possibilities obliterate their predecessors.

The notion of context is thus "impure", derived through an empirical process involving comparisons with elements from the history of the architectural response to spatial situations. It is an operational notion, a tool within the project process, a way of taking in the world, a perspective enhanced by theoretical precepts; it brings attitudes and general intentions in line with the specifics of the given situation. It maintains a dual nature in raising and exploring issues regarding both physical and mental materials, figures and anthropology. It resists any definition that would require it to be applicable to any of a variety of different situations and produce the same results. It exists and preserves its original fertility only if exercised continually and repeatedly; it lives and breathes only as an ever-active element in the project dialogue.

Once it began to be a commonplace, the principle of context lost some of its initial innovativeness and interpretive problematics, running the risk of becoming a sort of cover for ordinary practices. Driven by a banalized historicism to seek out architectural characteristics that would represent a form of memory, it has, at times, fallen back on normative crutches, shrinking from the more demanding exercise of judgment, reducing the objective of coming to terms with the characteristics of a given setting to a predetermined procedure and the art of architecture to an applied practice.

Housing design is especially caught up in this drift. For centuries now, the concept of habitation has implied a condition of stability. The dwelling-place, almost completely ignored in architectural treatises, first became an item of interest in medieval registries, then a subject treated in manuals, and in the twentieth century acquired a specific centrality linked to social ideals of liberty and equality. In the second half of the century, the notion of "pre-existing environmental elements" gained epistemological value for its contemplation of urban history as a problematic palimpsest and reference source. But all too soon, the simultaneous emergence of the question of historical centres versus peripheral zones, and obsession with historical memory versus the extirpation and dissolution of public space, initiated a slow shift in the notion of context toward banal mimicry of the pre-existing both in terms of style and height, reducing the question of dwelling-space into generic considerations of "urban fabric". Context was thus reduced to mere surroundings, which are attributed unimpeachable value as such. In the meantime, the quest for new housing types deviated into an assessment of purely quantitative, performance-oriented aspects and the demonstrative potentials of large public works were sacrificed before the altar of pre-established norms. What often prevails is a general defence of the characteristic reduced to inscribed stylistic notations; the contemplation of the fit between building type and urban morphology is abandoned, as are the strategies for undertaking the urban design project as a dynamic interpretation of complex interacting spatial systems. Habitation thus loses the temporal depth that characterized its evolution in association with changes in society and the family, and in our conceptions of hygiene – or rather, changes in the representation of the human body and in the dichotomies of proximity-distance and promiscuity-privacy.

The current horizon of urban redevelopment seems to bring a variety of issues back into play. Above all it clearly highlights the relativity of the projects: that which can be done amounts to only a small part of what already exists, thus spurring and opening spaces for thought about temporal depth and the evolution of processes. Exemplarity thus loses its clearly demonstrable characteristics and enters a system of relations that are both predetermined and modified by the project process itself. The multiform variety of the urban space seems to acquire a new centrality precisely at a time when the very idea of redevelopment should also spark a critical look at the pre-existing elements. Otherwise all is reduced to a mere question of replacing old buildings. Contemporary urban redevelopment plans, including the most recent experiments with neighbourhood contracts, embody a richer complexity of planning and design where even the relationships between public and private works are shaped around an idea of collective interest, demanding projects that are innovative both architecturally and economically, as well as the development of adequate financial instruments to fund them. The social and functional multiplicity achieved as mechanical forms of monofunctionalism are superseded re-evokes a continuity with the long historical process undergirding the construction of the European city.

The standard administrative instruments – including land registry maps to certify measurements and property rights, and the terms "ground floor" and "lots" for development, to name just a few – allude merely to the project's relation with civil and administrative law more than demanding any intentionality on its part. The jargon term "footprint", on the other hand, represents an idea of rootedness, of a broader critical evaluation of the urban space. It reproposes a space of propinquities, a space at human eye level, as the crucial spatial and temporal dimension in the relationship between public and private spaces. In this space, distance takes the form of a path and emptiness loses its abstract features. Empty space becomes a meaningful dimension that orients one's perception, and the regulation of the public-private relationships loses its heavy juridical connotations and begins to take on figurative ones. The placement of things on the ground along with the landscaping plan emerge as strategic and foundational acts, as an original form of attributing measurements to space. Here space is no longer indifferent, but instead organized into a system of relations embraced and transformed by the project, which thus opens itself up to being judged and historicized. The section is not merely for "control of overall building and floor heights", but a specific form in the design process for evaluating interrelations, an interpretation of the contextual conditions, an investigation of the relations between inside and outside that contribute to determining building type and layout, and spatial arrangement. The extended section encompasses landscape design and building orientation.

Age-old questions are reproposed with the specific intention of preserving the operational vitality of the notion of context, so that it may continue to challenge the techniques of the architectural project and its paradigms, seeking to prevent any innovation of the project from being reduced to the mere certification of numerical performance data and architecture from being reduced to procedural aspects where the distinction between ends and means is lost.

Auer+Weber+Architekten
Philipp Auer,
Dominik Schenkirz

Eso Hotel on Cerro Paranal

2002
Cerro Paranal, Chile

The European Southern Observatory operates the Very Large Telescope on the Cerro Paranal, a mountain in the northern part of the Atacama desert in Chile. Beneath the summit, at a height of some 2,400 metres, lies the hotel for the ESO scientists and engineers who work here on a roster system.
For the relatively short time of their stays under extreme climatic conditions a place has been created far away from civilization where they can relax. Reminiscent of an oasis, it provides 120 hotel rooms, a canteen, and lounge areas, as well as a swimming pool, fitness centre and library.
The hotel complex fits snugly into an existing depression in the ground, acting as an artificial support wall. A single element of the hotel's structure is visible above the horizon: a slightly raised dome comprising a steel skeleton that measures 35 metres in diameter.

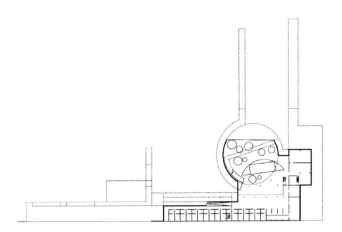

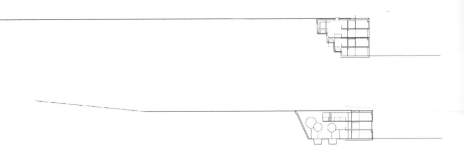

Ryue Nishizawa   **Moriyama House**

2005
Tokyo, Japan

The Moriyama House consists of six dwellings, one for the client and five freestanding apartment units. The plot is located in an attractive part of Tokyo where the traditional Japanese urban atmosphere still remains. Such an arrangement of volumes enabled us to determine the size and shape of each individual room freely and to provide every home with a small garden.

Various characteristics were given to the units, such as a three-storey unit with a broad sky view, a squared shaped unit half-buried in the ground, a unit with a very high ceiling, or a unit surrounded by gardens in all directions, and also diverse exterior spaces were created, such as small enclosed gardens or alley-like spaces. We sought spaces that do not close themselves into the interior but spaces that flow from the interior to the garden and alley.

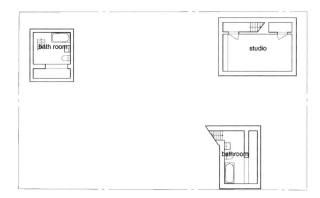

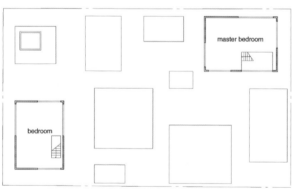

master bedroom

bedroom

bedroom

study

library

bathroom

roof terrace

void

void

Gigon/Guyer Architekten
Annette Gigon,
Mike Guyer

Broëlberg II

2001
Kilchberg, Switzerland

The complex is located in the eastern part of Broëlberg Park in a hollow
between the old mansion and a villa built in the 1950s.
Different types of apartments reflect the different qualities and features of
the site. The cores for stairs, lifts, kitchens, and bathrooms are space-defining
elements determined by the structural engineering and the installations
themselves. They structure the living areas, which can be additionally subdivided
with dry walls, thus allowing individual arrangements, from traditional rooms
to an undivided space defined only by the cores and sliding walls.
Being closely linked to kitchen and living room, the glazed loggias become focal
rooms in the apartments. On the ground floor they access an outdoor patio
and on the top floor large outdoor terraces.

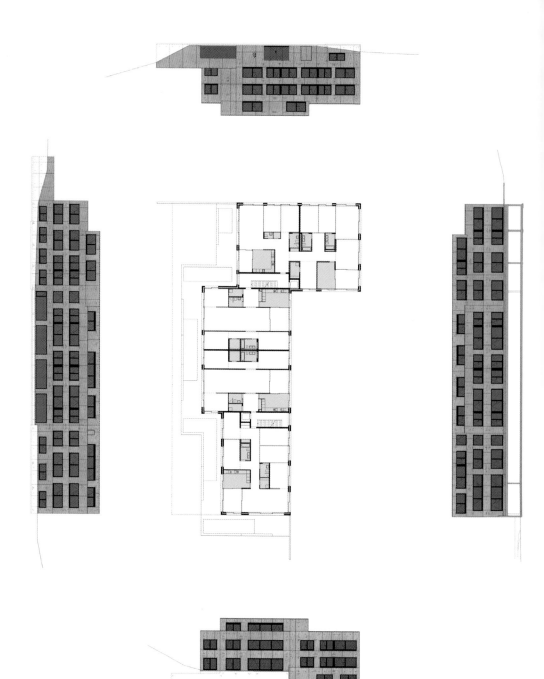

CZA
Cino Zucchi

Former Junghans Industrial Area

1996–2003
Giudecca Island, Venice,
Italy

The urban layout of the project recognizes in Giudecca Island the presence of two heterogeneous scales: the one of the dense fabric on the north side of the island, and the more sparse one of the industrial precincts overlooking the Laguna.

The project performs a sort of "microsurgery" in the former industrial area, alternating deep transformations (by refurbishment or new construction) and slight modifications of the existing buildings with open spaces. The former Junghans precinct is thus opened up to the city, creating a new outlook toward the extraordinary Laguna landscape. New paths are opened in the gaps between the industrial buildings, a new channel is excavated, and a new square bordered by the existing school garden generates a long view toward the south.

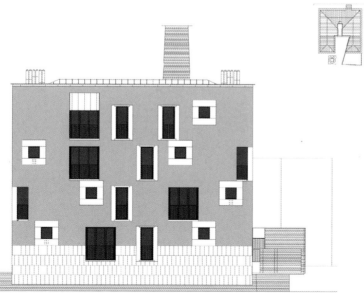

Housing Kloostertuin Apeldoorn

2006
Apeldoorn,
The Netherlands

A leftover plot on the edge of a Vinex-area in Apeldoorn forms the site for 52 dwellings. The dwellings consist of 32 semidetached houses, 10 detached houses and 10 single row houses in order to meet the diversity of market demands. Despite the big differences in housing typologies, there is a strong coherence. A unity is formed, composed of a big diversity, where every dwelling has its own maximum spatial qualities. The sloping roofs that create an alternating image formulate an iconographic aspect within the entire complex. The skew line creates the entrance of the house, whereby shelter is given when it rains. There is a conscious choice for an abstract appearance based on traditional typologies. The materialization of the black slate and the stone facade give this abstract appearance a natural character.

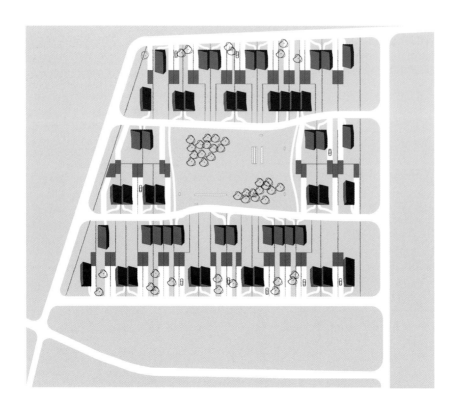

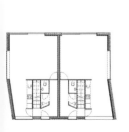
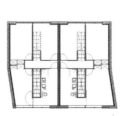

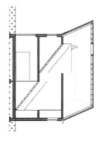

Camillo Botticini
Giorgio Goffi

Aler Houses

2004–05
Castenedolo, Brescia,
Italy

Located at the margins of the historical centre of Castenedolo, the building
extends along an old stone wall that once enclosed the property of the nearby
palazzo of a noble family.
Each one of the five small apartments, built using cost-saving methods, is
composed of a living room with kitchenette, a bathroom and a bedroom. The
sequence of these components creates two small courtyards. The first creates
physical and visual continuity between the indoors and outdoors, with the living
room opening outwards through a generous window, while the second is an
accessory space accessible from the kitchen area.
The use of bricks with flush, coloured mortar lines and Siberian larch for the
storeroom blocks and the canopies repropose the characteristics of local rural
architecture in a non-imitatively historicist interpretation.

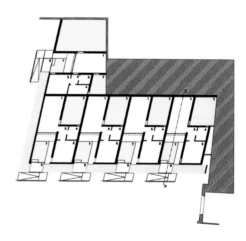

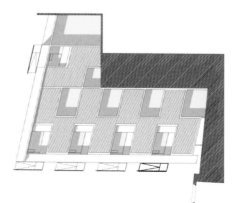

Pietro Carlo Pellegrini   **Progress, Residential Complex for 55 Units**

2005
Lucca, Italy

The urban context for the complex is an area of small artisan workshops and stores undergoing transformation on the outskirts of Lucca and currently characterized by a lack of any significant architectural works. The new building rises from the remains of an abandoned industrial complex, whose old brick smokestack, the only landmark of any architectural value, has been conserved as a memento of the past.

Two low towers of irregular shape stand on a rectangular base and from them jut small cube-like balconies. The two towers abruptly conclude their upward rise at the protruding eaves, which decisively put a halt to the verticalism of the architecture and reintegrate it with the base slab. The walls with their light grey stucco are embellished with mosaic glass decorations in various shades of purple that engage in a relationship with the planarity of the substrate: they dig into it, they cover it over or they detach themselves from it in a dynamic interplay.

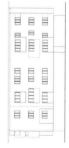

PEEP: 10 Row Houses for a Housing Coop

2008
Ventoso di Scandiano,
Reggio Emilia, Italy

The Low-Cost Popular Housing Plan (*Piano per l'Edilizia Economica Popolare* – PEEP) has restricted the footprint and the sequence of the ten units in the three residential blocks. The shared design elements of the ten dwellings have generated significant modifications to the formal aspect of the project. Instead of the usual housing style, characterized by an underground garage, the external carport was preferred, allowing a flexible and complete use of the garden. The dwellings make optimum use of the top floor under the sloping roof, offering views of the surrounding hilly landscape.
In the horizontal plan, the simplicity of the distribution system favours the personalization of the interior spaces. In elevation, the variety of the openings marks out the rhythm of the compact buildings, characterized by the use of grey fibre-cement and white clinker brick.

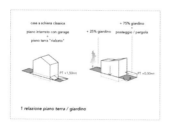
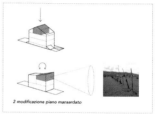

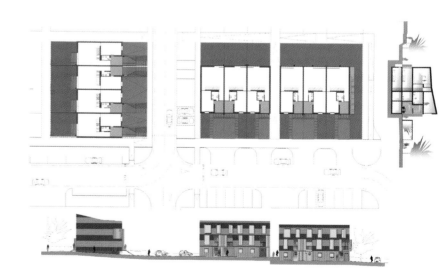

Helena Paver Nijric   **Housing Complex**

2004
Rovinj, Istrian peninsula

Fighting against the sprawl in the suburban context of Rovinj, the housing complex is designed as introverted and compressed. The compact solution of the entire system is immediately inverted by the roof and colour discontinuity. One very important part of the project is the common spaces, which are designed as galleries, semi-open spaces which remind of the Mediterranean way of life, that of narrow streets and small squares which wait for the inhabitants to colonize them. These galleries play with colour, texture and light in order to become a space for interaction.
Each apartment has a loggia, which becomes an outward sign with its coloured surface.

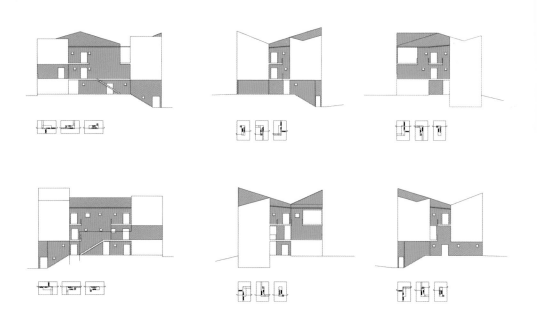

Residential Development

2004
San Bartolomeo,
Reggio Emilia, Italy

The new development is located in a newly urbanized area. It entails eighteen units organized into two apartment blocks and six row houses.
The "ingredients" imposed by the client (low apartment blocks and row houses, facing in bare brick, *coppi* tile roofs…) are "dehydrated" and recomposed according to new principles: the logic of real and visual pathways, which cut into and traverse the volumes and give shape to the ground floor portions; and the rationale of the views, which emphasize the environmental qualities of the surroundings in a configuration of spacious loggias.
From this derives a tension between heaviness and lightness, which is articulated through the suspension of a uniform and tangible mass upon a smooth and set-back base, and the incision of the mass with measured setbacks and deep recesses.

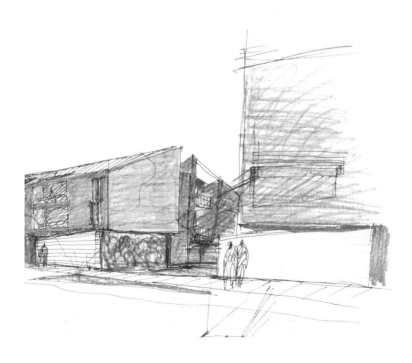

Claus en Kaan
Architecten

Fisherstraat Housing

2003
The Hague,
The Netherlands

In this urban renewal project in the Transvaal district of The Hague, the building line and closed form of the old block were maintained. Typological diversity is hidden behind a uniform skin punctured by large window openings. The long sides consist of single-family dwellings with ground-floor storage spaces on the street side. One short end consists of apartments, the other of four-storey townhouses with a roof terrace. Underneath is a car park for eighteen cars. Another, slightly sunken, parking area is located behind the gardens in the narrow yard of the shallow block (only 36 metres in all), thereby satisfying the demand for a percentage of off-street parking.

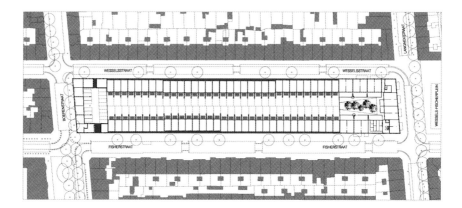

Hans Kollhoff
Helga Timmermann

Leibnizkolonnaden

2001
Wielandstrasse 19–22,
Leibnizstrasse 49–53,
Berlin, Germany

Measuring 32 metres by 108, the new urban square between the Wielandstrasse and the Leibnizstrasse is an oval space defined and delimited by the typical Berliner curtain of buildings surrounding it, giving it the characteristics of metropolitan space often found in large European cities.
This urban space lined with restaurants and cafés is completely free of automobiles. In the summer months, the square hosts a variety of public events. A fountain concludes the square toward the Leibnizstrasse and isolates it acoustically from the street sounds. Two-floor colonnades amplify the square, offer shelter in inclement weather and constitute a fine boundary-line between the shop areas and the public space.
The buildings, eight stories high at the maximum, contain apartments, shops and offices.

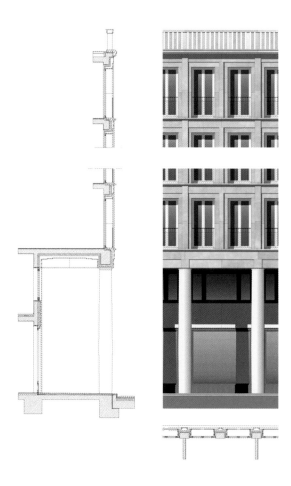

2001
Java-Eiland, Amsterdam,
The Netherlands

The existing old buildings of the shipping companies all face outward toward the quay. Toward the inside, to each other, they remain unconnected. The two planned buildings are designed to place these disparate parts in relation to each other.

Viewed from a distance, the two projected buildings lead the row of the two "superblocks" of the neighbourhood to a striking conclusion. The long building placed directly at the water's edge differs in site and volume from the two residential blocks whose built volumes circumscribe the courts. The courtyard building occupies a central position in the transitional area. Its volume seems to be simultaneously in the sway of static and dynamic forces. This act of balancing continues into the apartments which are not hierarchically organized. It is a residential building that should also allow life outside traditional family structures.

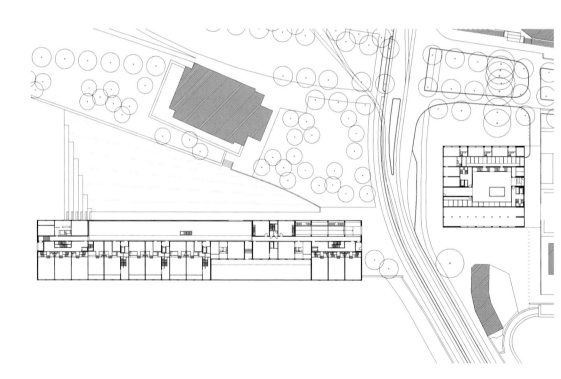

Ufficio Progetti
Architetti Associati
Bertani e Vezzali

Single-family Houses at Canali

1998–2003
Canali, Reggio Emilia,
Italy

The project involved the construction of five dwellings in two distinct blocks connected by a portico. The north unit contains two dwellings while the other one has three. The two central units of the residential complex are outfitted with a small apartment on the ground floor for use by family members. These spaces were conceived to ensure flexibility and adaptability to different lifestyles.
The three units were designed with a single family in mind. The spaces on the ground floor have been organized as studios or summertime dining areas.
A simple system of shutters, partition walls and loggias or porticoes offer privacy and shade where exposure to neighbouring eyes and direct sunshine demands it.
Each unit is outfitted with a patio that opens the residential floors in a vertical sense, bringing light and greenery into the depths of the houses.
Bare bricks are used for the walls, cedar wood for the shutters, Cardoso stone and sandstone for the floors of the loggias, and flat and *coppi* tiles on the roofs.
External walkways are paved in brushed cement.

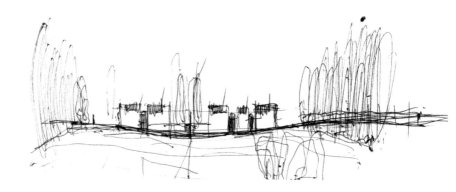

Sergio Pascolo

Siedlung Alfred-Delp-Weg

1st phase 2003,
2nd phase 2006–07
Göttingen, Germany

The project involves 105 low-income dwellings within the Zietenterasse, a redevelopment area of former military barracks and the site of residential expansion on the city outskirts. The volumetric definition of the project correlates closely to the architectural and typological solution: three building units are placed on the long and narrow lot, each one composed of an assemblage of modular "parcels" measuring 17.4 metres on a side. With the design of their roofs, their serial character creates a compact, monolithic structure that re-establishes an urban rapport between building and street while still conserving characteristics of individuality that enhance the inhabitants' sense of identification with their personal dwelling.

The structure of the units has been designed to create flexible dwelling types to satisfy a diversity of needs and lifestyles, with the maximized neutrality of the spaces ensuring the broadest range of use options.

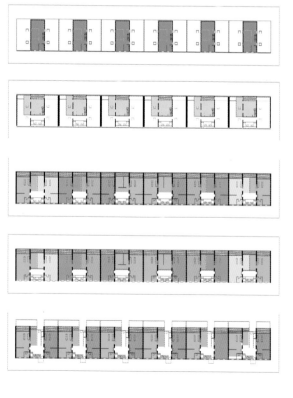

Cristofani Lelli Architetti   **Houses in Via Campana**

1995
Faenza, Ravenna, Italy

The complex of ten row houses is characterized by a collective central space circumscribed by the facades of the two opposing building units, creating a cosy interior space. This sense of intimacy is enhanced by the fact that it is an exclusive pedestrian area that gives access to the main entrances.
There are no separations between properties inside and this unity is echoed by the continuity between the walls and the full-height doors and windows made of multilayer okumè plywood and solid niangon wood.
Private drives give access to the gardens of each house, where the facades are characterized by loggias embellishing the openings to the interior rooms and whose concrete baffle bearing structure and partition walls in oxidized iroko strips create semi-enclosed exterior spaces.

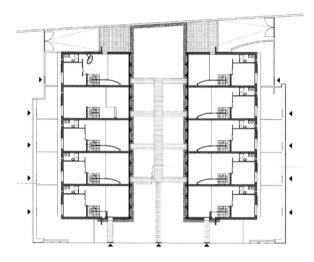

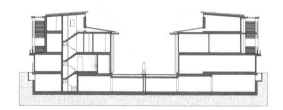

Claus en Kaan
Architecten

Ter Huivra

2003–04
Joure, The Netherlands

Ter Huivra is an eighteen-apartment building, with office or retail spaces on the ground floor and a car park basement, and it is situated next to the natural landscape of Ter Huivra parkland. Maximizing the views to this landscape and its orientation towards the sun sculpted the building's form. The fluid curves are emphasized by the generous cantilevered decks. These decks provide both for wide access galleries and private outdoor living spaces. Placing the car parking underground frees the building from the visual impact and the remaining open space of the site is sheltered by the building itself, creating a defined outdoor room. A restrained palette of materials: white steel slab edge and balustrading, white framed glazing, with a wooden terrace floor, ensure the building maintains a strong and clear horizontal character.

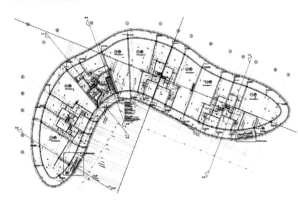

E2A - Wim Eckert,
Piet Eckert, Laurent
Brunier, Nicole Manser,
Pascal Mumprecht

Broëlberg Housing Complex

2002–03
Kilchberg, Zürich,
Switzerland

The project is based on a horizontal striation formulating three antithetic
architectures with four conceptual horizons: a sunken base containing all
infrastructures, a free span living plan on ground floor, a chamber work
of individual rooms on the upper floor and an open summer house on the
roof garden relate the different spatial configurations similar to a vertical
selectively used menu of living. The structural regime follows the vertical
differentiation and expresses on the upper floor a continuous concrete
beam, bridging the spans on ground floor.
The design provided a rigorous location for democratic divisions with vertical
layering, ensuring that everyone would have an equal relation to the park.

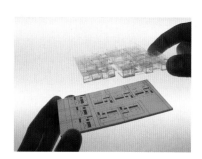

Inhabiting

Inhabited Screens. "Individual" and "Standard" in Contemporary Housing
Cino Zucchi

Sleeping, washing, studying, preparing food, putting things away, resting after work: the units of activity contained in the circles of functionalist diagrams were supposed to reform the human dwelling to meet objective and universal needs, opposing the morality of the *Neues Wohnen* to both the social hypocrisy of the middle-class home and the squalor of the slums of the industrial metropolis.

But the list of needs that the modern dwelling must satisfy now has to be updated in the light of the new desires and lifestyles of the variegated population of city users. If the rationalist manuals contained the stylized dark outlines of a "standard" humanity (abstract typical users consistent with the resources of the new clean and sunlit accommodation), designs for a contemporary dwelling ought perhaps to contain the icons of the diverse virtual population of Second Life or the Sims. The concept of the custom-made, of "personalization", now appears to have brought together the body, the clothing, the domestic environment and even the musical, literary and artistic tastes of residents, transforming the walls of the house into an existential niche governed by the unquestionable individual choice made possible by the "dropdown menu".

The "liberation of desire" of the 1960s has lost its political overtones and instead taken on a commercial character, generating a broad range of niche market targets by ever more aggressive advertising, where the slogan of "do your own thing" is paradoxically used to promote the products of global brands.

Whether they like it or not, contemporary projects for housing carry in their genetic code many of the results of functionalist and postfunctionalist research into mass housing. Ironically, however, the principal ideological presupposition of this research, that of an egalitarianism in the positivist mold stemming from the "universal" character of human needs, has been dropped.

In recent architectural competitions on the theme of housing, complicated periodical tables of the elements or gene maps lend ideological support and a dubious scientific basis to porous residential structures, where the model of the Japanese Metabolism movements, Yona Friedman or Moshe Safdie's Habitat 67 in Montreal is subjected to a further atomization to allow for increasingly idiosyncratic lifestyles. Prophetically, the image of the great viaduct conceived by Le Corbusier for the plan of Algiers, where an infrastructure running through the landscape teems with the facades of houses in the most eclectic styles, presages the more carefully controlled research carried out in the 1970s by John Habraken and published in *Variations*[1] (the name could appear on the cover of one of the voluminous tomes produced by a generation of young Dutch architects, attesting to the underlying cultural continuity between the MVRDV and Hertzberger's generation), where the distinction between support and infill was supposed to ensure the necessary balance between unity and variety of the urban scene.

But the extreme "democratization" of housing proposals for the contemporary metropolis is now taking on new harmonic overtones, entering dangerously into resonance with the parallel targeting of market niches by advertisers or the entertainment industry, in the obsession with originality and personalization that characterizes the ever greater diffusion of commodities in mass society.

May the city live long, notwithstanding the after all not so original existences of its inhabitants! Today an awareness of how the city survives individual destinies seems to be the only way of thinking that is capable of laying the foundations for an ethic of resistance to the consumption of the ever-changing images of that "sex-appeal of the inorganic" described by Walter Benjamin.

"Architecture has always represented the prototype of a work of art the reception of which is consummated by a collectivity in a state of distraction. [Its] appropriation is accomplished not so much by attention as by habit",[2] declared Benjamin, who elsewhere urged us to "live without traces".[3] Going back to a vision that is in some ways conventional of the relationship between container and content – not so different in the end from the progressive "loftization" of residential space – might constitute a healthy antidote to the suburban atomization of the fabric that used to make up much of the city we love.

However, the conflict between housing and city, between the right to individual expression and the conservation of public space – which echoes other typical conflicts between the playful use of the city and the not-in-my-backyard attitude – can perhaps be resolved today through techniques of "mediation" or the simple creation of an "interface". Form arises everywhere there is a need for communication: we could see form as the necessary "translation" between one system and another, which allows two adjoining realities to hold a dialogue and represent each other.

The movement of the body, which traces and carves out the empty envelope of its living space (from Alexander Klein's diagrams of minimum routes to the organic interior of Kiesler's Endless House), does not appear capable of producing true sociability, nor of true evolution over time of the building substance generated by it. Better perhaps to imagine inhabitants as hermit crabs, in empirical emigration from one shell to another through the orderly trails of the housing ads.

In this sense, the landscape of the *Interieur* – from the elegy of the Biedermeier to the protoplasm of Ikea – is not capable of confronting the city directly without destroying it, like a cancerous cell that knows no boundaries and hierarchies among parts. It has to be confined by osmotic membranes that regulate the exchange between the two environments: windows, terraces, balconies, walls, parapets and screens that create microclimates of transition between outside and inside. Thus Coderch's large house-shutter at Barceloneta constitutes the common ancestor of many mutant species that have appeared in the urban ecosystem in recent years, collective organisms capable of joint action against the "suburban plankton".

"With this shift from the transparent form to the opaque one an opposition between interior and exterior is born that does not exist in transparent organisms. [...] The surface of the animal, now opaque, is turned into a new organ; with it a new two-dimensional reality emerges, largely independent of the structures inside. A surface of this kind is not just a 'frontier', a shell that serves to protect the internal environment or safeguard the metabolism, in short a mechanical means of defense, but is transformed into an organ with completely new possibilities. [...] The opaque surface takes on a value of its own as a showcase of optical phenomena. [...] The opaque surface makes it possible to establish relationships."[4] The "skin" described by the biologist Adolf Portmann appears to be aware of its own independent value and its own semantic powers. The functionalist tradition, in a hypertrophic aspiration to "sincerity", denied independent formal value to the facades of houses, restricting them to an, in some ways, ingenuous expression of the organization of the interior. Contemporary designs put new formal configurations into effect that aspire to the aesthetic paradigm of camouflage, so widely used in modern fashion, which is increasingly adapting the functional prostheses of the body (watches, sunglasses, military accessories) to play a "cosmetic" role.

In opposition to the panoptic ideal of the glass house, inhabited by tidy demigods, we now have interiors without a face; or perhaps it would be better to describe them as the "ephemeral screens, looking as if they slide" that Raffaello Giolli saw in the urban architecture of Asnago and Vender.[5]

If a cautious experimentalism characterizes the "foundation cities" of the new docklands or the Northern European polders like IJburg in Amsterdam or Wasserstadt in Hamburg, the transformation of large disused industrial zones in Italy into residential areas has for the most part been based on a few, disappointing real-estate models.

While it is true that the happy period following World War II can still offer useful lessons on modern living in the urban setting, it is not even remotely possible to solve the problems posed today by the constantly changing environment of the multiethnic metropolis with the sunny model of the "functional city" capable of integrating urban fabric and open space.

But the lesson of the housing project is also one of humility and seriousness, in an age that favours formal hyperbole even in the absence of meaning; it requires an attentive, affectionate gaze, one that knows how to work by means of small shifts rather than grand proclamations, pursuing a coherent series of small variations that can lead to unexpected discoveries. Of the new house, of the new city we would like this, the fact of being at once reassuring and unexpected, capable of articulating the space of relationship and protecting the private dimension that Christopher Alexander saw as a primary necessity in defense of contemporary homogenization.

Void or ether? Today the question of the form of the common space between housing units appears to be suspended between different objectives. If the modern tradition's policy of the "district" sought to re-create the social solidarity of the village within the new urbanized class, it is not clear what ought to be the social model or the formal paradigm of the connective space of contemporary residential fabrics. The monolith and the carpet, the Unité d'Habitation and the Horizontal City of Diotallevi and Marescotti, echo continually in contemporary housing projects, which often seem to have renounced the reassuring urban icons of the postmodern period. But an agitated and continual variation, like in the carpets of sound woven by the compositions of Philip Glass or Michael Nyman, erodes the egalitarianism maintained by the paradigms in order to pursue the ambiguous relationship between affirmation of the individual and standardization of that immense ideal "middle class" on which Western social democracies are founded.

Perhaps only the confrontation with the "different", with the implantation of non-European social customs within the European city-territory, can undermine the all too orderly sequence that has already integrated the varied experiences of "participatory planning" for some time now. If photographic images of Eastern cities indirectly reveal the failure of the modern ideal of a "rational" beauty of the big city, the European city may need to metabolize better the mosaic of subcultures which increasingly characterizes it, accepting into its well-organized body those vital anomalies that bring the metropolitan dimension to life, according to the prophetic words of Josef Frank: "So the new architecture will be born of the whole bad taste of our period, of its intricacy, its motleyness and sentimentality, it will be a product of all that is alive and experienced first hand: at last an art of the people, not for the people."[6]

[1] J. Habraken *et al.*, *Variations. The Systematic Design of Supports*, Cambridge (Mass.) and London: MIT Press, 1976.
[2] W. Benjamin, *Das Kunstwerk im Zeitalter seiner technischen Reproduzierbarkeit*, Frankfurt am Main 1955; Eng. trans. *The Work of Art in the Age of Mechanical Reproduction*, New York: Schocken Books, 1968.
[3] W. Benjamin, *Einbahnstrasse*, Frankfurt am Main 1955 and 1972–89; Eng. trans. *One-way Street and Other Writings*. London and New York: Verso, 1979.
[4] A. Portmann, *Aufbruch der Lebensforschung*, Frankfurt am Main 1965; Eng. trans. *Essays in Philosophical Zoology. The Living Form and the Seeing Eye*, Lewiston (NY): Edwin Mellen Press, 1991. The passage has been translated here from the Italian ed., *Le forme viventi. Nuove prospettive della biologia*, Milan: Adelphi, 1969, pp. 23–24.
[5] R. Giolli, "Architetture che fanno quadro," in *Costruzioni-Casabella*, 191–192, November-December 1943.
[6] J. Frank, *Architektur als Symbol. Elemente deutschen neuen Bauens*, Vienna: Verlag Anton Schroll & Co., 1931.

Residential Buildings at the Portello

2003–05
Portello, Milan, Italy

The portion of the redeveloped industrial area east of Viale Scarampo designed by Cino Zucchi Architetti calls for five special-lease residential buildings, three open-lease residential buildings and one office building.

The grand scale of the pre-existing industrial enclosure offers an occasion to reformulate the relations among the parts via the creation of new routes and pathways establishing the circulatory system for the area and reconnecting it with its surroundings.

"While today's real estate reality tends to repropose tried and true building types with little interest for their setting within the city", states Zucchi, "our project seeks to create a series of new high quality collective spaces that draw the city dimension into dialogue with the scale of the single dwelling. [...] Research into the environmental needs of the contemporary dwelling is combined with contemplation of the best residential construction following World War II and its capability to be grafted onto the pre-existing city."

Calori Azimi Botineau
(CAB) Architects

Beausoleil

2004
Beausoleil, France

The project is located in Beausoleil, a small town between Nice and Italy, built
on the hillside between the sea and the mountain.
The apartments are placed from level one upward. The ground floor and the
basement are utilized for naturally illuminated and well ventilated car parks.
Nine conduits punctuate the length of the building. These form double-aspect
apartments articulating around blocks composed of kitchens, bathroom
and toilets. Originally designed as two or three-roomed apartments, they can
be coupled together to expand the interior volume and the central units adapted
to new desires. The final two levels are comprised of three adjacent duplexes,
considered as villas on the roof, each having the benefit of a panoramic solarium.

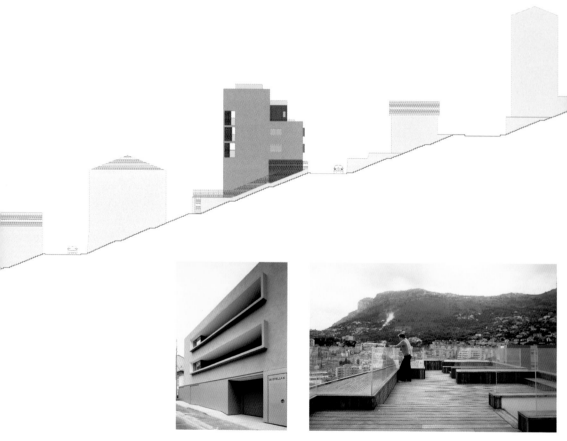

David Chipperfield
Architects

Villaverde Housing

2005
Madrid, Spain

The housing scheme is located on plot 203 of a new development district of
southern Madrid. Comprised of 176 one-, two-, and three-bedroom apartments,
the scheme responds to an overall masterplan for the site, which requested
a single U-shaped block, 15 metres deep, and with a footprint of just over
2,000 sq.m.
The increase in floor area achieved by this reduction in roof volume also allowed
for a more sculptural approach to the building envelope – carving back the sides
of the block, away from the orthogonal, to create a more varied outline to the
building's elevation.
Further distinguished by its choice of materials – earthy-pink concrete facade
panels, a rich dark grey concrete for the courtyard portico, and a dense band of
landscaping in between – the effect is a rich tricolour radiating outwards.

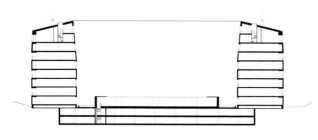

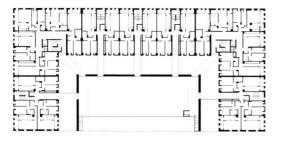

MGM Arquitectos
José Morales Sánchez,
Juan González Mariscal

99 Viviendas Sociales

2001
San Jeronimo, Seville,
Spain

While keeping dwelling dimensions to a minimum, the project seeks to expand the space, constructing a sort of filter of some 12 sq.m between the indoors and the outdoors. The spaces are arranged along diagonals and offer views of the garden, onto which the apartments look via a system of projecting elements. A sense of permeability is achieved by ample transparent elements: on the first floor a sliding glass partition is the only element that separates the domestic space from the garden.

The building comprises a mixed structure in order to allow greater availability of surface for openings. The doors and windows are set into cut-outs in the structure. The surfaces are faced in galvanized steel panels that resolve the problem of rainwater collection and waterproofing of the roof.

Headquarters of the Wohn+Stadtbau Housing Association

2002
Münster, Germany

Entering the city from the north, a straight road, at the apex of its perspectival triangle the silhouette of a cathedral and other church towers. Progressing into this picture, slightly downhill the view is gradually obscured, the outer traffic ring crossed.

The next 500 metres rise, not a dramatic topography but enough to awaken expectation – "up there I will be in the city". Buildings on the right enclose and to some extent counteract the latent drama of this ascent, this arrival. The left is undergoing a transformation, a re-configuring, a chance for a modulated roofline to enhance topographic character.

This is the intention of the sculpted silhouette of the new offices of the Wohn+Stadtbau Housing Association.

MVRDV   **The Silodam**

2002
Amsterdam,
The Netherlands

In the western part of the Amsterdam harbour an expensive urban operation
has been undertaken in order to densify the city and to meet the demands
of the market, even on one of the more vulnerable areas. A former dam with
a silo building has been transformed into a new neighbourhood.
A mixed programme of 157 houses (to buy or for rent), offices, work, commercial
and public spaces had to be arranged in a 20-metre-deep and 10-storey-high
urban envelope.
These houses differ in size, cost and organization. In order to accommodate
this process in time, a series of neighbourhoods of 8 to 12 houses have been
created: blocks of houses that surround a corridor, a garden, a gallery, and a hall.
As a result, an unexpected sequence of semi-public routes appeared: from
galleries on one side one can walk via openings and corridors to galleries
on the other side and higher up. Connecting all the houses with the hall, the
public balcony, the harbour, the barbecue, and garden, a three-dimensional
neighbourhood materializes. It became a container of houses, literally
interpreting the surrounding harbour.

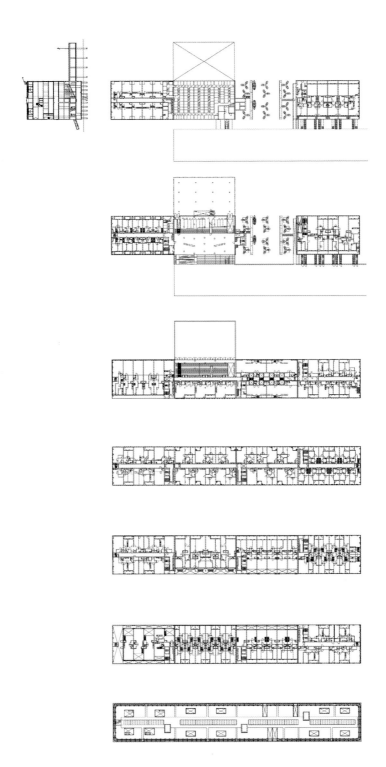

Beckmann-N'Thépé
Agency

ZAC Masséna

2007
Paris XIII, France

Based on the principles designed by Christian de Portzamparc, the project emerges, develops, takes shape to enhance its simplicity with its own specific elegance.
The facade overlooking the street extends in strict alignment like a cheesewire.
The overhangs, the recesses, the compositions of terraces and a crevasse structure emphasize the blocks forming this architectural complex, allowing the neighbouring buildings to benefit from the "open island hub" of the development plan.
The facades unfold like a large graphic composition, generous and scaleless.
The notion of floor levels is concealed, the rhythms of the openings are systematic and surprising. The inside is echoed by precise, nearby or far-off frames, profiting from the panoramas offered by eastern Paris.

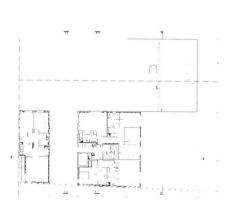

Andreas Fuhrimann
and Gabrielle Hächler
Architects

Apartment House at the Foot of the Ütliberg

2003–04
Zürich, Switzerland

The task was to create a reasonably priced residential space with high standards of living comfort for four differently sized parties.

In the process, each party was to profit as much as possible on the one hand from the 3,000 sq.m south-facing environs, and on the other from the north-facing view over the city. This determined an unconventional and complex internal organization of the building. All four apartments are accessible via a two-storey entrance hall. In principle, the two double-storey apartments and the two roof apartments are encapsulated in each other so that the quality of the four-sided building is fully exploited. In addition, one of the roof apartments also has access to the garden. Commonplace materials such as concrete, timber, wood and galvanized steel were chosen, which, when combined, animated each other.

Guido Canali

Red House on the Lungoparma

1971
Parma, Italy

The Red House appears as a blocky, dense volume, typologically reminiscent of the early twentieth-century buildings that flank it. Filled structural volumes form a secondary facade on either side and accentuate the frontal corners. The views from the apartments are strongly oriented: open in a long view towards the river and the opposing facade, and closed toward the neighbouring buildings. The openings are buffered from the traffic and the beating sun by loggias, some deep. The project offers an occasion to reflect on the language of bare brick. Although smooth and produced in a most elementary and spare rendition by industrial extrusion, the bricks create compact, monolithic walls rising directly from the flower beds. In terms of composition, they allow greater liberty, tending toward abstract architecture and precise planes.

Hans Peter Wörndl
Max Rieder
Wolfgang Tschapeller

Housing Complex

1999–2001
Salzburg, Austria

The project consists of two housing blocks that contain a total of forty-eight dwellings. The facings of the T-shaped row of houses, in an architectural style that lies somewhere between industrial and domestic, make the construction stand out from the otherwise classical urban landscape of the city. Two long bays divide the lot into two equal rectangles, serving to evenly distribute the apartments, which have either one or three floors.

The wood theme complements the outdoor planters that create a wooden side terrace, extending the interior space into the outdoors.

Prefabrication of construction elements – such as the concrete parts, the wooden facade and the membrane that wraps the building – was decided with the aim of making the project more cost-effective and cutting down construction time.

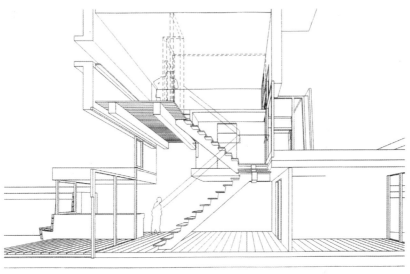

Rue des Suisses Apartment Buildings

1999–2000
Paris XIV, France

Our two apartment buildings on Rue des Suisses are incorporated in their urban context, typical of housing blocks in many Parisian *arrondissements*. Our buildings, with their undulating facades and folding shutters, fit seamlessly into the vertical arrangement of the frontage.

We tried to realize a model for living that is relatively unusual in the centre of Paris: instead of competing with the towering fire walls, we settled on a horizontal strategy, that is, we kept the buildings low to ensure that as many flats as possible would be directly and intimately connected with the grounds and the garden.

An extended, three-storey structure with arcade-like balconies forms the backbone of the complex in the interior of the block. Adjoining it are cottage-like, one-storey buildings for the kitchens and bathrooms. In front of the long garden wall that runs along a school playground, we built a few extra small, one-family homes with gabled roofs. The result looks like a seemingly random system of small units, courtyards and lanes with fragments of old and new walls covered with cultivated and wild vegetation.

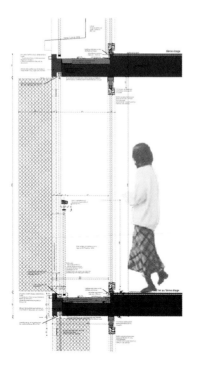
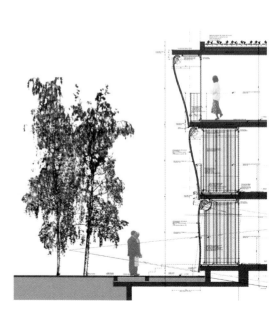

Carlos Ferrater
Xavier Martí

Vertix

2007
Barcelona, Spain

On the new Diagonal in Barcelona, facing the park designed by Jean Nouvel at the end of the northern arm of the city block, there is a residential building that meets the twofold requirement of overlooking an open Cerdá Plan block while standing alone as an autonomous element.
Six apartments per floor are distributed along a zigzagging corridor that links the two vertical communications cores.
The apartments are provided with intermediary spaces obtained through the interleaving of the different rooms, and in which sliding blinds are distributed on the inner and outer face, thus maintaining privacy and light control while helping to achieve open spaces that link the exterior and interior of the dwellings.

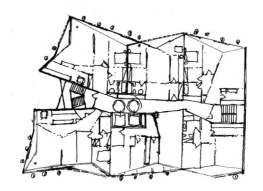

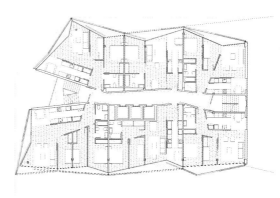

Pietro Carlo Pellegrini   **Blue House**

2002
Sant'Anna, Lucca, Italy

Situated on the outskirts of Lucca, the building stands on a long and narrow lot and completes work begun in 1997 on the construction of twin residential buildings. The apartment layouts and building plan are regularly arranged and complete the grid of the pre-existing urban fabric. The facades are tinted with colour fields that delineate and inform the crisp box-like structure. The blue parallelepiped resulting from this is animated by panels in glass enamel mosaic that mark out the rhythm of the windows. The canopy that shelters the building entrance is a sort of accent that stands out sharply against the flatness of the facade. The building is crowned with a delicate raised roof reaching upwards in asymmetrical dynamism.

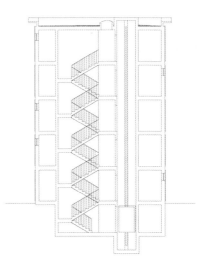

Cherubino Gambardella **Golden Palazzo**

2005–07
Montesarchio,
Benevento, Italy

At the intersection between Corso Caudino and the road to Benevento, there stood a concrete skeleton that was slated to be redesigned to house shops, apartments and offices. The project became an occasion for giving definition to a strongly urban architecture of significant monumental impact, almost a combination of city gate and building for the town's historical centre that is set in dialogue with the profile of the fortress and with the pre-existing elements in the urban environment, giving new qualities to the section of the city it looks over. The choice was made to swathe the frame in calculated proportions and design an armour of rusticated ashlars. From the base plane to the large cornice, which echoes the theme of the hanging cantilever, the facade is animated by light and shadow and edges. A golden mantle covers the travertine base in precious highlights, transforming the palazzo into a scintillating and enigmatic expression.

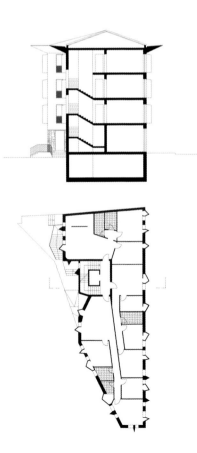

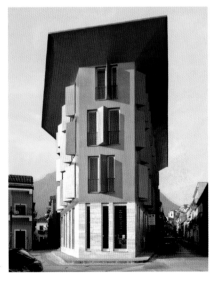

Erick van Egeraat
Harry Kurzhals

12 Apartments

2002
Mauritskade,
Amsterdam,
The Netherlands

The new building completes the corner of a nineteenth-century city block in the Dapperbuurt area in Amsterdam. It contains commercial space and an automatic parking system on the ground floor and twelve apartments on four floors above. A mix of vertical and horizontal lines were chosen for the elevations both to match the existing nineteenth-century buildings and to allow panoramic horizontal windows on the corner.

In plan, the floors at the corner slightly overlap each other creating an interesting play of volumes and shadows. The elevation is dominated by two kinds of different dark coloured natural stones with broken and sand blasted surfaces. Painted timber window frames are combined with a coated metal sheet in aluminium colour, which, due to the bend at the corner, reflects the sunlight in different ways.

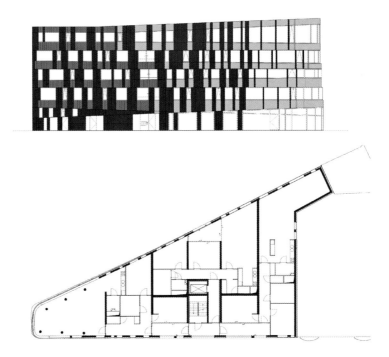

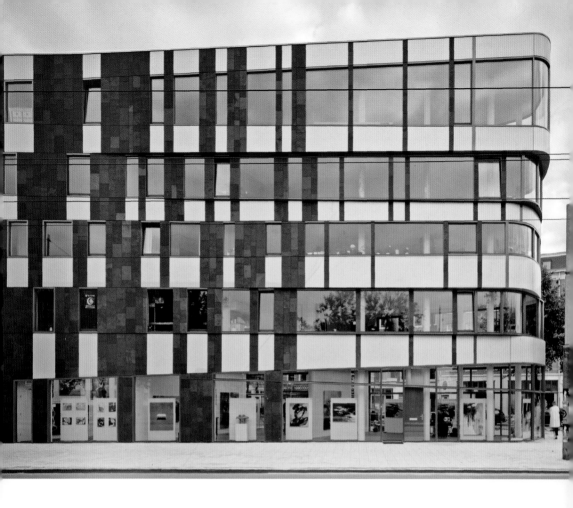

Riken Yamamoto
& Field Shop

Residential Complex Codan Shinonome

2001–03
Shinonome Koutou-ku,
Tokyo, Japan

Block 1 is composed of 420 units, two 47-metre high towers, and a 34-metre tower. Residential units are located in the upper floors. The assembly room and small offices are located on the second floor deck level, facing the large plaza on the artificial ground, and commercial activities, children's club and other facilities to support urban living are located on the first floor along the S-shaped avenue. There are numerous variations in the types of over a hundred residential units. The lifestyle of urban dwellers varies so much that a conventional residence cannot meet the functions they desire. Units with a "foyer room" are proposed as areas that can allow for such variations. The terrace that opens to double-height spaces in places through the residential tower allows light and air into the centre corridor, helping achieve both a high density and good living conditions.

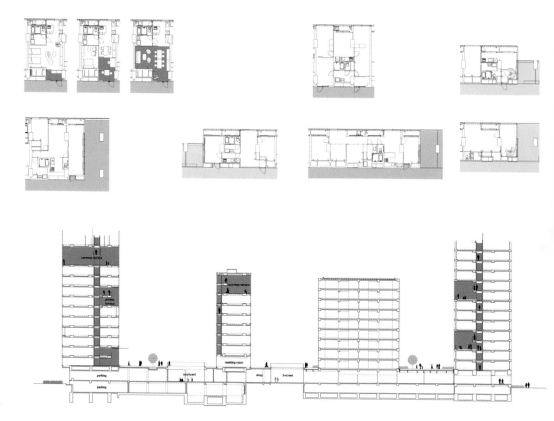

Claus en Kaan
Architecten

Apartment Block

2001
Oostelijke Handelskade,
Amsterdam,
The Netherlands

This apartment block, containing sixty-six subsidized rental units and six "DIY" units, is one of the many new buildings going up on the Oostelijke Handelskade in the former docklands district of Amsterdam.

Three sides of the industrial-looking building are composed of storey-high, precast elements of sand-coloured concrete, a uniform grid that serves to conceal a great variation in floor plans. The north facade is of glass and behind it are galleries lined by the entrances to the apartments. Halfway along the galleries are the stairs and lifts. The warm red and orange colours of the walls behind the glass compensate for the dark northern aspect.

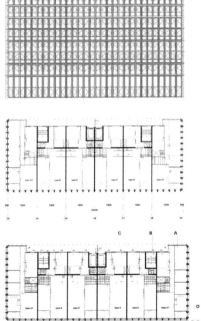

Massimo and Gabriella
Carmassi
with Guido Leoni

University Housing in Parma

2001
Parma, Italy

A long, narrow, slightly curving building contains 215 student apartments, each one measuring 40 sq.m and composed of a living room-dining room giving onto a balcony, a double bedroom and a bathroom with shower.

Some have external aspects with full height loggias supported on cylindrical steel pillars. One of the stair towers is incorporated into a large courtyard with *ballatoi* or elevated walkways, creating functional permeability between the two sides of the building.

Two cylindrical courtyards, located on either end of the paths crossing the park, constitute social foci for the housing project. To the northeast they are marked by a series of widely spaced, narrow, full-height openings that provide illumination for the elevated walkways, and by a series of wider openings that provide access-ways to the ground floor and outward views from the upper floors.

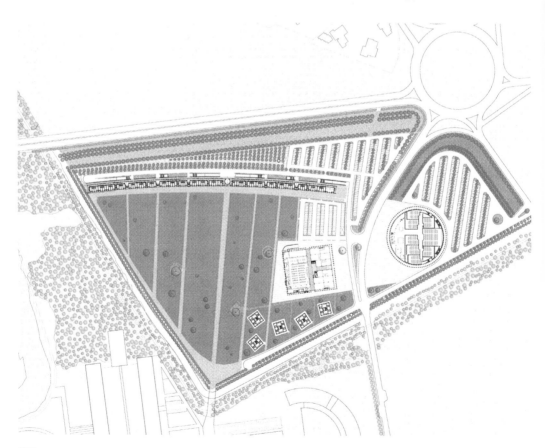

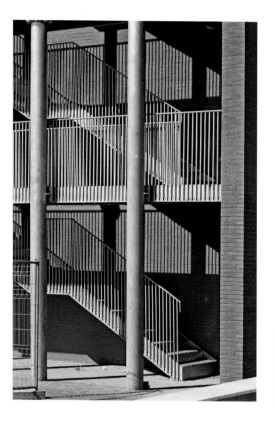

Breevaarthoek

2001
Gouda, The Netherlands

Breevaarthoek occupies the site of Rutgesterrein, where the peat moors meet the city. The project adapts to its environment, adjusting its form to the surrounding conditions with regard to sunlight, access and water views.

The triangular site encouraged a division into three sections: to the south, the short edge of the triangle faces the road with an apartment building. The other two sides of the triangle consist of low-rise drive-in dwellings, connected to the water's edge. These two edges are divided into water dwellings and garden dwellings. Here, landscape references are employed throughout, such as the wooden landing stages at the edge of the water.

The apartment building is the project's urban face. It contains twenty-three apartments and two penthouses and acts as a noise barrier between the adjacent road and the dwellings behind.

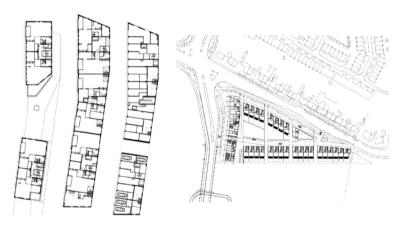

Housing Development

2002
Ypenburg, The Hague,
The Netherlands

This project is part of an archipelago in the The Hague and is based on the urban development schedule of the architectural office MVRDV. In this project we have searched for an alternative to the typical row in which houses are usually grouped. The design consolidates houses into ensembles situated around a courtyard.

From the outside the blocks of houses look like one big house. The houses are of different dimensions, which cause an alternating pattern of buildings with open spaces in between.

Two "big houses" have been adapted for eight group dwellings for mentally and physically disabled people. The dwellings are situated on the north side of the plan, separated from the Landingslaan by water.

The interior design has been determined by the limited mobility of the inhabitants. Each group house has its own layout and its own colour that determines the interior.

Block of Flats in Rua do Teatro

1995
Oporto, Portugal

When, in the eighteenth century, Oporto grew beyond the Medieval walls, the peripheral estates were subdivided and developed in long, narrow lots, adapting to the topography of the land. The houses, also long and narrow, were built with prefabricated elements in sculpted stone, thus defining the openings almost *a priori*. The remaining parts are generally faced with *azulejos* for the main facade, metal sheet for the secondary facade, and slate for the sides.
This edifice follows the same tradition in the construction principle. The stone structure is replaced by iron girders, while the facings are the same, in zinc and slate.
The transformations in architecture are not so rapid and evident as it would appear in the manuals.
It is necessary to pass through the drawing and construction phases in order to reach normality.

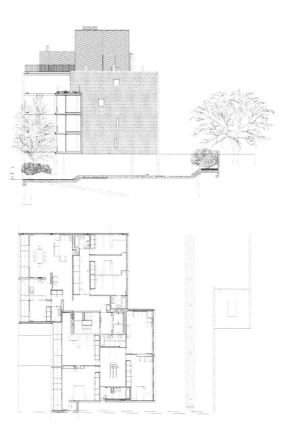

Apartment and Office Building

2001
Barcelona, Spain

The 11.60-metre wide party-wall building exhausts the whole of its buildable depth extending from the chamfered corner to the interior of a city block. The programme is developed on four residential levels, with two apartments er storey; and three basement levels for parking organized in part floors. The facade is structured using vertical elements with a fifty-fifty mix of solids and voids, as is compulsory in the Cerdá Ensanche, and it consists of four onion-like skins 40 cm in thickness: an interior curtain wall of glass with a full-height modular form, apertures with struts of nyangon wood sliding on runners, a running balustrade with slim steel fasteners and frames supporting stone slabs of silver quartzite from India collocated in 90 x 30 cm horizontal sections with 4 cm openings which coincide with the empty sections of the porticoes.

Calori Azimi Botineau
(CAB) Architects

Strip of 6 Apartments

2006
Eze, France

The landscape demanded a rapport with the building and the architecture was
thus approached accordingly. The entry to the residence was designed with
consideration to the horizon line and suggests an extended *belvedere* prolonging
the public space toward the panorama.
The project is composed of two units: the three "duplexes" are anchored in
the grounds to the west and the three "simplexes" perch on top of the car park.
The apartments are placed forming a strip and are connected and served by
an open air corridor, which, for the duration of the approach to the entry doors,
offers a respite from the horizontal views, instead of framing the sky above,
and glimpses of the neighbouring scenery. Each residence profits from a private
connection to the exterior utilizing two typologies: a loggia as extension to the
living room surface and a generous rooftop solarium.

Benedetto Camerana
& Partners,
Benedetto Camerana
(lot 4, group leader)
Studio Rosental (lot 4)
Steidle und Partners
(lot 3)
Derossi Associati (lot 5)

Olympic Village for Athletes, 2006

2003
Turin, Italy

The buildings are generally six or seven floors high with some eight-storey units and others of three or five stories as connecting elements along the main facade. The spaces on the ground floor along the main avenue are used as offices for the Olympic Committee. The large windows on the streetfront and the nearly continuous window sections giving onto the internal garden enhance the sense of transparency and minimize the structure's visual barrier effect.

One of the fundamental features of the project, winner of an international design contest, is the strong presence of colour, conceived within a relationship between contemporary art and urban architecture. The Berlin architect Erich Wiesner conceived an architectural coloration project using eleven contrasting colours.

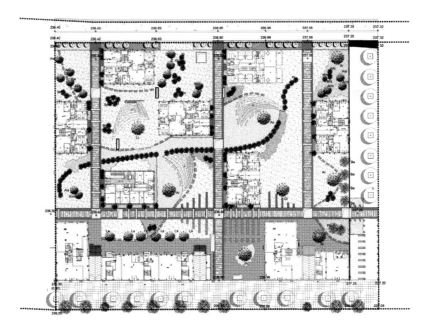

Manuel Aires Mateus
Francisco Aires Mateus

Students Housing, Campus II

1999
Vila Franca Pinhal de
Marrocos, Coimbra,
Portugal

The new students housing of Coimbra University and the campus canteen
are located between a sloped vehicular street and a horizontal pedestrian street.
Together they define a tilted triangular space, on a beautiful topography.
The triangular sloped morphology of the site is reflected in the organization of
the lower levels of the building. A tower rises from this platform. The programme
consists of student bedrooms, grouped in pairs with shared living rooms. In the
tower, bedrooms face east to take advantage of the view; on the ground floor
they are placed on the south. Walls are of two types: the blind ones are made
of split concrete blocks with a precise measure that defines the height of the
construction; walls with windows are clad in wood panels that integrate window
portals in their dimensions.

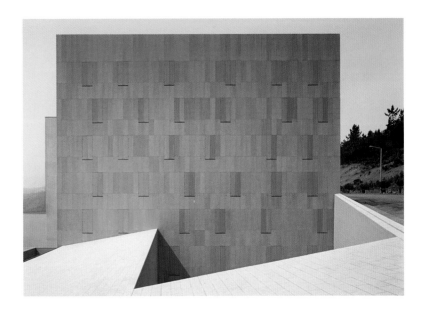

OFIS - Rok Oman,
Špela Videčnik
with Martina Lipicer,
Nejc Batistič,
Neža Oman,
Florian Frey,
Marisa Baptista

Social Housing

2004–06
Izola, Slovenia

The brief required thirty apartments of different sizes and structures, varying
from studio flats to three-bedroom apartments. There are no structural elements
inside the apartments, thus providing flexibility and the possibility of reorganizing
things. The project proposed a veranda for each apartment, thus providing an
outdoor space that is intimate, partly connected with the interior, shady and
naturally ventilated.
A textile shade protects the balcony and apartment from prying eyes, yet due to
its semi-transparency allows the owner to enjoy the views of the bay. Perforated
side-panels allow summer breezes to ventilate the space. The strong colours
create different atmospheres within the apartments.
The small rooms become visually bigger because the textile shade creates
a perspective effect that connects part of the exterior with the interior.

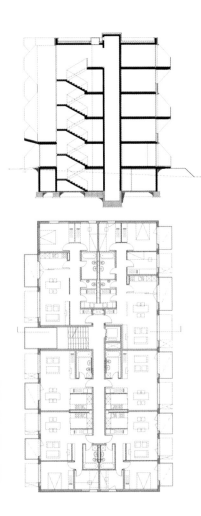

Reinhabiting

Reinhabiting
Pietro Carlo Pellegrini

Honouring the memory of a place and valorizing existing industrial facilities provide both stimuli and opportunities to architects.

Projects to reutilise older structures offer the possibility of experiencing the old and the new at one and the same time. The conservation of historical buildings by seeking out new ways to use them can establish a new equilibrium and give greater creative tension to the redevelopment project.

A project that takes form on the basis of pre-existing structures illuminates the strong connection between past and present, between history and contemporary daily life. A reading of the past is superimposed upon and integrates into contemporary reality. Knowledge of the constituent elements of the historical building and its relationship with the urban context constitute the point of departure for the formulation of guidelines to shape the project.

The pre-eminent characteristics of the historical complex guide the choices in the reuse project: the system of residential spaces is harmoniously insinuated into it, establishing new relationships and equilibria with the functional plans, the interior distribution schemes, and the architectonic and structural elements.

The project thesis addresses the recovery of the historical identity of the built complex through the rediscovery of historical values and their relevance within the tradition of the city, so that they can become the generative elements of the contemporary project while at the same time being reshaped and redefined by it.

"Architecture can modify the way we live, it can act on a person's behaviour and become, itself, a sensor for discovering and updating the new arrangements of the city. The strategies for action must be conceived within a design process that is both dynamic and independent, thus achieving an 'undertone' mutation of the entire urban system. We can think about flexibility in the city using ideas that constitute a system of liberties, measured by means of a value set that shall recognize the tool of planning and design as an element for forecasting the overall development of the city and its ongoing relationship with the surrounding territory."[1]

Architecture seeks to reinterpret and fulfil the various life needs of its users. In cases where old buildings are reused, the project also takes on the objective of giving new life to the existing structures in a harmonious way. And it does all this while seeking to transpose the themes of sustainable design into restoration work as well: reducing energy demand in existing buildings through performance improvements in building shells and the use of renewable resources; enhancing security conditions, dwelling quality and environmental compatibility.

The path of renewal becomes not just an occasion for getting better acquainted with our artistic, crafts, and industrial heritage; the quest here must also lead us to a renewed interpretation of the discipline of architecture, crafting it as a tool for the transformation and invention of new places that succeed in redefining the existing equilibria between interior, exterior and public spaces.

In cases where the new function given to the building is residential, there are even more variables brought into play in the project: the forms of historical architecture are reshaped to meet specific needs of domestic life, becoming humanized, shedding the aura of austerity that often distinguishes these facilities when they are converted into museums, libraries or other types of public spaces. We have grown used to this latter type of "refunctionalization" over the years. At the same time, however, the strong constraints imposed by the specific characteristics of each historical building (the dimensions of its spaces and their distribution, the materials of which they are made...) can be an opportunity to rethink the forms of the inhabited space itself, breaking away from certain established criteria and standards which had been seen as comfortably preordained.

For the same reasons it becomes difficult to devise a project methodology that can be reapplied. This is precisely because of the specificity of each project area, and it stimulates instead the quest for ever-new solutions in response to ever-different issues.

Architects like Lapeña + Torres, in their reuse projects, intervene in the existing with a light and elegant touch, revisiting the architecture of Josep Antoni Coderch in the interior spaces, and in the design of the details. Just take for example the iron staircase created for the Mas House in Barcelona.

Miralles + Tagliabue, in the La Clota House, again in Barcelona, combine maximum flexibility of spaces with the recovery of original structures, which become sculptural elements giving definition to the domestic spaces.

Umberto Riva recovered a single-family dwelling in Milan, the Frea House, designing a space characterized by transparency and wooden interior walls, which trace out the plans of the different floors and merge into the language and detail of the internal and external doors and windows.

Remaining in Italy, we can find an analogous attitude in the works of Guido Canali and Danilo Guerri. Their designs are different, but also rich in complex simplicity, details and harmony, transparencies that cut across the recovered spaces of the past.

John Soane's House in London on the other hand stands as a model for its light, colours and proportions. It is "a house as an identity card. [...] Centimetres fitted around our skin and our eyes that never succeed, not even together, in registering everything that this house, bursting with energy, can still teach us today".[2]

[1] P. C. Pellegrini, "Flessibilità", in *Multiverso*, 2, 2006, p. 22.

[2] B. Finessi, "Lezioni di architettura degli interni", in *Abitare*, 474, 2007, p. 65.

Massimo Carmassi

San Michele in Borgo Residential Complex, Pisa

1985–2002
Pisa, Italy

The complex is a renovated city block that had been partially destroyed during World War II. It is composed of three units which enclose three sides of a new quadrangular piazza, with the fourth delimited by the apse of the adjacent church. To the north, the pre-existing wall has been completed with a series of setback arches, while to the east it was rebuilt on the remains of the Medieval foundations by means of two layers of bricks used as permanent formworks for the poured cement core.

The east lot contains a unitary volume on the ground floor with shops and five apartments looking out onto the piazza from the upper floors. The panels that separate the fissures from the volumes ensure fluidity between street and piazza. On the ground floor level they are made of steel and glass. On the upper floors they are made of larch panels that screen the openings with their retractable shades.

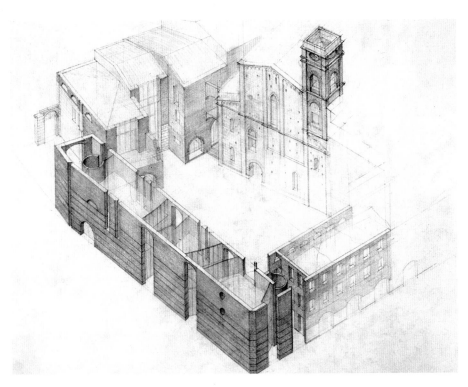

Valeriano Pastor **Dwellings at the Former Iceworks**

1993
Giudecca, Venice, Italy

The dwellings are built within a system of strata generated by the remains of a seventeenth-century palazzo and the old iceworks.
The new building is made of bare brick that is distinguishable, on the basis of the qualities, laying technique and form of the bricks, from the old walls, which have been partially restored via the use of recovered brick.
The project is composed of 23 apartments for 71 people. Its layout is based on a *calle* (Venetian street) shaped like a bayonet with two narrow strips of houses. The new *calle* provides access to the dwellings with some of the living rooms and bedrooms giving onto it. The decision to preserve the wall of the icehouse – a sign of pre-existing production activities – as a bearing structure gives the *ballatoio* (a long balcony giving access to several dwellings from the courtyard) status as an independent architectural unit, a vantage point on the remote past of the icehouse and its continuation through a receptive architectural expression.

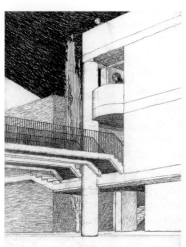

UN Studio
Ben van Berkel
with Olaf Gipser

Addition to and Partial Renovation of the Hotel Castell

2004
Zuoz, Engadin,
Switzerland

Great attention was paid to the placing of the building volume, its proportions
and relationship to both the Castell's impressing monolith nearby and the
dynamics of the picturesque landscape. While corresponding to the volume
inflection of the existing hotel, its facade relates to the soft flow of the
topography with a transformation between open and enclosed balconies,
structuring the entire building as tectonic formation of shifting horizontal strata.
In order to capture the stunning panorama, the south facade is entirely glazed
and affirms the building's modernity in contrast to the adjacent Castell.
Considering each dwelling's spatial and visual exposure towards the surrounding
landscape, the floor plan layout has been kept open and simple, allowing for
a flexible arrangement of spaces around a fixed central core.

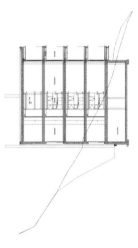

C+S ASSOCIATI
Carlo Cappai,
Maria Alessandra
Segantini

1=10, The Bishop's House

2008
Fognano, Brisighella,
Ravenna, Italy

The Casa del Vescovo (Bishop's House) is a structure standing in a park among cedars of Lebanon. The building underwent general restyling to carve out ten small apartments. The longest side of the building faces the street and, together with the adjacent church, creates a sort of small city access gate to the centre of Fognano, while it offers views out of corner windows on the side giving onto the park.

The use of materials and colours from the local tradition enters in harmony with the surrounding landscape while the structure still maintains its role as a building within its context: a double architectural order on the upper part is imposed upon the pre-existing base.

The utility system was designed to produce a building with low energy consumption requirements.

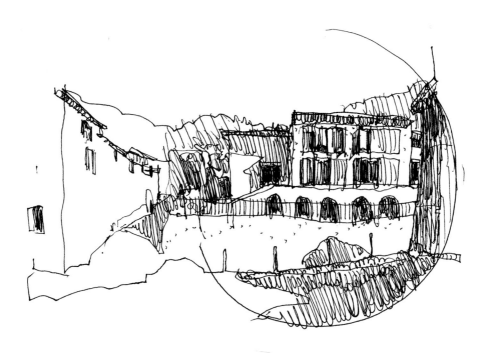

Gonçalo Byrne

Residential and Commercial Complex

2001
Chiado, Lisbon, Portugal

The project addresses a group of eight buildings in the high district of Chiado from the irregular central courtyard they enclose and circumscribe.
The architectural plan is laid out along two penetrating axes crossing the block and accommodating the commercial component, which is lodged in the ground floor units at the different elevations, both toward the street and giving onto the courtyard. The new characteristics of the slightly elevated space of the internal garden reconfigure the courtyard as a public space. Together with the access-ways to the shopping area, the public space opens up the view of the garden and of the bell tower, which were previously hidden from sight.
The upper floors accommodate residential units and offices in separate areas. The sublevels are almost all dedicated to parking.

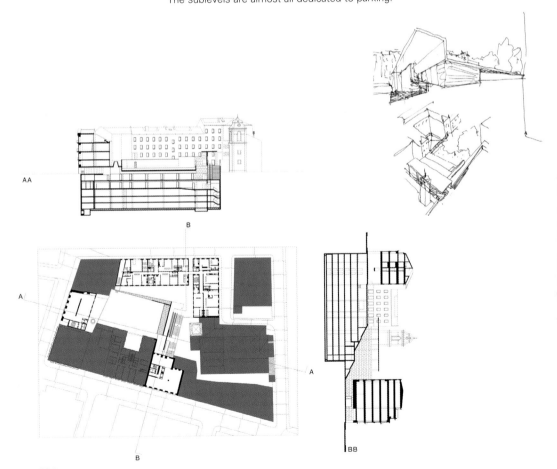

AA

B

A

A

B

BB

Palazzo Gioberti

2003
Turin, Italy

The project entails the reconfiguration of the highest floors of the historic building
by superimposing a completely new element on it. The residence is situated
on the rooftop level and has its own flat terrace roof.
The pre-existing design with stepped-back floors is emphasized by the redesign
of the external surfaces. The surfaces have no openings on the facades, are faced
in opaline methyl acrylate panels and treated like a unified system of recessed
loggias onto which the interiors open. The facing of the facade thus becomes the
liaison between the historic building and the new structure. Contemporary
ornamentation, seen in surface details and effects of light, is juxtaposed with
that of the past, composed of friezes, stucco decoration and columns.

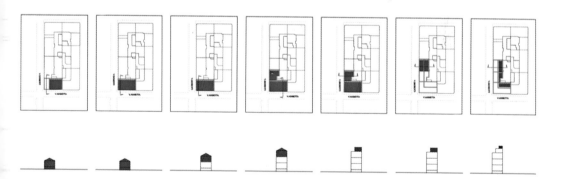

Gasholder Housing

1999
Vienna, Austria

The Vienna gasholders were built between 1896 and 1899; thus all four gasholders were disguised as buildings by means of enclosures of brick walls topped by glass domes.

The project keeps the enclosure intact as a testimony of its times and designs a series of segments which house apartments on fourteen levels. These inner "buildings" are slightly detached from the original wall so as to provide for vertical accesses. The shopping centre which links the four gasholders is covered here with a glass dome and surrounded by planters with grass.

The inner space is clearly the main facade: each segment has access to outside views through the windows in the brick wall either directly or across the inner space between the segments.

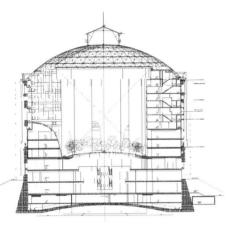

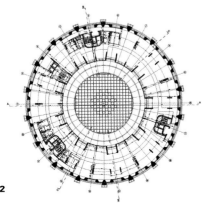

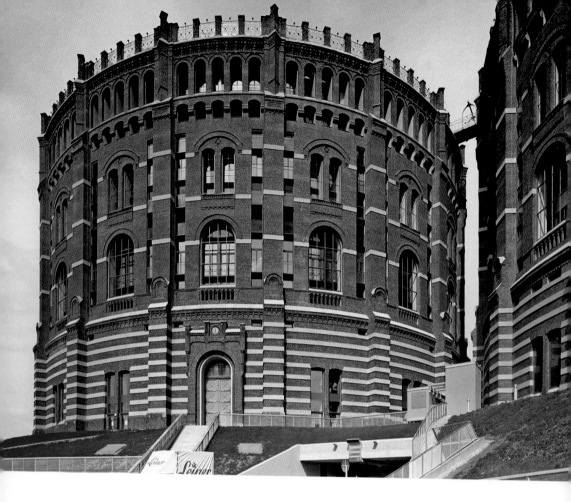

Gasometer B Apartment Building

2001
Vienna, Austria

The specific location of these gasometers within an industrial site as well as the unusual character of the resulting spaces led to the gasometers often being used for diverse cultural activities.

The concept of the Gasometer B adds three new volumes to the existing facade: the cylinder inside the Gasometer, the striking addition of the shield that is visible from outside, and the multifunctional event hall situated in the base of the Gasometer.

Inside the cylinder and the shield are apartments and offices. The 360 apartments offer differentiated living forms, ranging from three-room-maisonette-apartments and loft-apartments to smaller ones like student apartments. By combining office and apartment uses, new ways of working and living are expected to emerge.

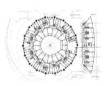
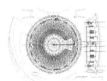